KRUGER NATIONAL P

MAKE THE MOST OF KRUGER

Jacana

Johannesburg

Acknowledgements

The Kruger National Park and Jacana Education
are deeply indebted to the individuals and organisations
who have made this publication a reality.

Created by
The Kruger National Park and Jacana Education

DTP Origination: Jacana Education, Johannesburg,
Lithographic Repro: Remata Bureau, Johannesburg,
Printing: Fishwicks the Printers, Durban

The publishers welcome any comments.

Published by
© Jacana Education Johannesburg 1993
P.O. Box 2004, Houghton 2041, Republic of South Africa
Tel: (011) 648-1157 Fax: (011) 648-5516
Second Edition 1994
Third Edition 1995
Reprint 1996, 1997

ISBN 1-874955-34-4

Foreword

The primary objective of National Parks is to ensure that unspoilt areas, representative of the broadest scope of the natural diversity of our country, are preserved. Furthermore, the most salient statement of intent in the mission of the National Parks Board is to preserve natural ecosystems in their most pristine state possible. This not only implies that the full range of animal and plant species, and their habitats, are protected but also that ecological processes, such as droughts, periods of high rainfall - and in many cases even disease epizootics - are allowed to take their course. National Parks are set aside to preserve nature for nature's sake. Everything that is inherent to nature, is important and worthy of protection!

But National Parks are not created to exclude visitors. On the contrary, National Parks are the natural heritage of the people of the country; they are the most treasured possession of all as they represent the base which sustains our development programmes and quality of life. Our National Parks should be the pride and joy of every citizen of this country!

To appreciate our National Parks in particular, but also our environment, (of which we are all an integral part!), we need to know more about the constituent parts of nature and the intricacies of the interdependence and interaction between them. Knowledge is the key to understanding, respect and appreciation. In turn, these virtues form the cornerstones of an environmental ethic - the sacred code that dictates attitudes, decision making and utilization.

Together with its obligation towards the preservation of ecosystems, it is also the stated mission of the National Parks Board to promote an environmental ethic. This it endeavours to achieve by making its National Parks accessible and affordable to the broadest possible spectrum of all South Africans (and visitors from abroad), and by providing the scope of experiences, opportunities and facilities to meet all tastes and pockets. In addition, it also encourages any form of audiovisual and literary projects of educational value. In this respect, it recently joined forces with Jacana Education to produce a new road map and information booklet, (*Find It*), for use by visitors to the Kruger National Park. These publications contain a host of extremely valuable information in "easy to assimilate" fashion and have consequently also proved to be highly popular with visitors. These publications have, in fact, added so much value to a visit to 'the Kruger' that it was decided to put them together in book form and make them available to a broader public through various outlets other than only the Kruger National Park. Anyone who has the interests of nature, and our National Parks at heart will benefit from this book and also feel the need to share it with their friends!

We trust that this publication will go a long way to instill an environmental ethic, and a love for our National Parks in all South Africans!

Dr S.C.J. Joubert
Executive Director:
Kruger National Park

CONTENTS

Ecozones 37

Find It 47

Glossary 89

Index 90

Notes 92

Welcome to the Kruger National Park

Kruger National Park is one of the few places on Earth where you'll find mammals, ants, birds and insects in their natural environment. The more you know and understand about the bushveld, the more pleasure Kruger will give you.
You will discover many fascinating facts in this unique book. Enjoy your visit!

Stretching almost 350 km from north to south and 60 km from west to east, Kruger's wealth lies not simply in its immensity, but also in its variety. The Park's roads take you through different, interesting ecological zones. The trees, the flowers, the grasses range as the kilometres pass and so do the rock formations, the river-beds and of course the animals and birds.

Kruger is here for you!

It is a National Park and therefore belongs to everyone. It is here for us to enjoy now and is a place that will be treasured by future generations. Whether you like relaxing so completely that you sleep through the lion's roar, or you study your guide book ticking each whisker and feather – Kruger is for you!

Look for these publications by Jacana Education. They are available in the following languages:

Make the Most of Kruger – English, Afrikaans, German
Bushveld Seasons – English, Afrikaans
Find It – English, Afrikaans
Visitors' Map & Travel Guide – English, Afrikaans
Living with the Land – English, Pedi, Tsonga, Zulu
Sappi tree spotting – English

In Nature, individual elements combine to form a greater whole.

The same principle applies to our products and services.

VOLKSKAS BANK

The bank you can rely on

Everything in Nature is linked ...

Sun ...

Rain ...

Geology ...

Plants ...

Animals ...

CARNIVORES
– eat flesh

INSECTIVORES
– eat insects

OMNIVORES
– eat flesh, insects & plants

HERBIVORES
– eat plants

Mammals, birds, reptiles and insects live where there is adequate protection and food and where they can reproduce successfully

TREES, SHRUBS, FORBS AND GRASSES

Types of trees and grasses differ according to variations in climate and geology

SOIL

Underlying rocks erode to form sands and clays. These qualities are influenced by their parent rocks

PARENT ROCK

Rocks formed over thousands of millions of years have unique mineral composition

Sun

Rain

As you spend time in the Kruger National Park read about the way that each element depends on the others.

Plants depend on water and the energy of the sun, as well as food in the soil, for growth.

Animals live by eating these plants or eating the flesh of other animals.

The waste products of plants, as well as the waste products of animals, feed the soil.

In the Kruger National Park there are many things that could interest you.

This book will help you to look in the right places, at the right time of day, to *find* more, and *understand* more too.

The species, and sites, described here are generally common, *easy to find and easy to identify.*

Enjoy the Kruger National Park and make the most of your visit.

5

How to make the most of this book

1 Study your *Map*

The *Maps* on pages 24-35 show 16 natural areas (Ecozones) in the Kruger National Park.

- ❏ Each Ecozone has its own combination of geology, land-shape and rainfall.
- ❏ This means that each Ecozone has its own pattern of vegetation and associated animals.
- ❏ Each Ecozone has been given a name, a specific colour and a letter, from **A** to **P** (e.g. **A** – Mixed Bushwillow Woodlands).

Which Ecozone are you in?

- ❏ Find your place on the *Map*.
- ❏ Identify the Ecozone that you are in – by colour and letter.

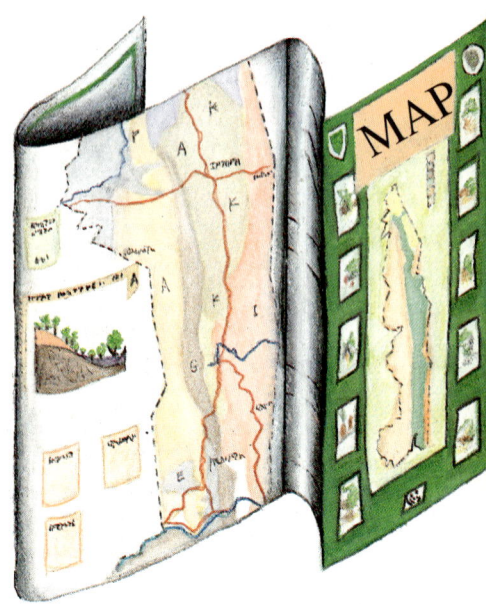

2 Find your *Ecozone diagram*

- ❏ Turn to the Ecozone section (pages 39-46) to find the colour-coded diagram of your Ecozone.
- ❏ The diagrams show you the species you can find in your Ecozone – i.e. which trees, grasses and animals are most likely to be seen there e.g. jackal berry and white rhino. (Note: The diagrams show where you are most likely to find the species, but do not indicate total distribution.)

3 Use your *Find It*

- ❏ This part of the book (pages 48-87) will give you further, detailed information about the species listed in the Ecozone diagrams.
- ❏ The *Find It* also gives you information about the geology and history of the Kruger National Park.

Throughout the *Find It* there are

Colour-coded headings

Next to the name of each species is a coloured "corner" like this which ties up with the colour-coded headings.

Colour used in this way groups species together which share a common feature.

> **Note:** These colours do not tie up with the Ecozone colours in any way.

---

4 Create a *Mental picture*

Look up the species and read all the information in the ***Find It*** section. This way you will be able to visualise the animals, birds and plants you are looking for in your Ecozone.

Find the answers to these questions:

❑ What do they look like?

❑ Where can you find them?

❑ What other information will help you find and identify them?

The following is an example of how to build up a Mental picture of .... White rhino .... Jackal berry

What does it look like?

❑ What shape is it? ....Study the picture..................Study the picture

❑ What size is it? ....1,8 m; 2 000 kg ....Up to 20 m

❑ What other species look similar? ....Black rhino.............................Tamboti

Where do you find it?

❑ In which habitat? ....Flat, open plains; short grass ....Riverine; termitaria

❑ In which Ecozones? ....**A, B, C, D** ....**B, H, M**

What other information will help you to find it?

❑ What does it eat? ....Grass

❑ Is it in a family group? ....Small group

❑ Does it have flowers or fruit?..........................Fruit: Sep – Oct

❑ Does it lose its leaves in winter? ....Yes: deciduous

5 Now go out into the bush and find it!

Be sure you are looking for the species in the right Ecozone and right habitat!

Keep this book handy and refer to the easy-to-read information regularly.

6 Once you have found the species – circle the Ecozone square!

❑ Throughout the ***Find It*** there are blocks next to each species. These represent all 16 Ecozones on the *Map* and are identified by the letters **A – P**.

❑ The individual squares that are **coloured** indicate the Ecozones where you are most likely to find particular species all year round.

❑ A few species are difficult to see because they are nocturnal. Their Ecozone blocks are entirely **grey**.

❑ Circle the relevant square as you identify anything of interest in that Ecozone. This will enable you to keep a record of each trip to the Kruger National Park.

❑ You should be able to circle most of the coloured Ecozone squares in the ***Find It*** as long as you visit the KNP during different seasons of the year.

A	E	I	M
B	F	J	N
C	G	K	O
D	H	L	P

Enjoy your visit!

7

Keep Kruger wild

- The Park is not only a refuge for animals and plant life – it is also a place for people. It is your National Park. Everything you do here affects the life around you. It is a great privilege, but it is also a real responsibility.
- A frightened animal can be very dangerous. Normally, they hardly notice visitors who watch quietly from inside their cars. But hooting, shouting, teasing or throwing things may frighten them, or even cause them to panic and react with aggression.
- It is vital that cars stay on the roads. Driving across any area that could be food or a home, could be destructive to the wildlife.

Vultures in the trees are often waiting for their turn at the kill.

White-backed vulture

Umbrella thorns

Wild date palm

Young lions sometimes battle to get sufficient food because of the dominance of the pride male. For this reason very few survive to adulthood.

Safety first

For your own safety and for the best game viewing, please be sure that no part of your body is outside your car. Animals are used to, and not afraid of, the outline of a vehicle. If you break the silhouette by putting your arm out, or your head up through a sunroof, they may become frightened and run away. Also, the animals in the Park are wild, and many are capable of biting – with serious consequences.

Nature deserves to be treated with respect and understanding.

A philosophy we extend to every one of our clients.

GENERAL INFORMATION

How to make the most of Kruger

Plan the practicalities

Kruger is a wilderness, rich with life, that has been kept as natural as possible. Between rest camps there are no petrol stations. Between picnic spots there are no restrooms or shops. You may only leave your car in areas marked on your *Map* with the symbol 🚗. Please read the checklist below before you set out.

Check gate and rest camp times

Like everything in the Park, these change with the seasons.
Please check on page 18 the times that the gates are opened and closed.

Use all your senses

Occasionally visitors to the Park are disappointed with how little they see.
This is often because they drive with their windows closed and hear nothing!
Yes, Kruger can be very hot at times. But you will experience so much more with your windows open and your air conditioner off. Most days it will be well worth the increase in temperature.
Remember to keep your windows closed when you're near monkeys and baboons. Near elephants it is wise to keep your engine running. Be very careful not to separate a mother elephant from her calf.

❑ Travel slowly   ❑ Stop often   ❑ Learn as much as you can   ❑ Relax

Checklist

Please, before you set off, be sure that:

- ✔ you have an up-to-date map
- ✔ you have enough to eat and drink inside the car
- ✔ everyone has used the toilet
- ✔ you have cameras, film, binoculars and litter bags handy
- ✔ your car has enough petrol

- ✔ no necessities have been left in the car boot
- ✔ you have bird, animal or tree books, and your copy of *Make the Most of Kruger* handy
- ✔ you have checked roads that are temporarily closed to visitors. These are listed on the notice board at reception.

Signs of an elephant nearby are newly broken branches, a tree stripped of bark, steaming dung, large wet patches in the road and tracks on the sand. Keep your ears open for breaking branches.

Kruger is unique

Millions of years ago a wide variety of animals, birds and reptiles roamed freely over every continent. Humans then became urbanised and dominant, and many of the larger, exciting mammals died out.
Africa is the only continent where a high concentration of a variety of species live naturally. The Kruger National Park is one of the largest of these sanctuaries. Kruger is not just here for the conservation of the wildlife, but for other reasons too:

Kruger is here for education

The Park is a vital learning centre. Many people come to understand the delicate balance between different cycles of life ... rain ... grass and leaves ... antelope ... carnivores ... vultures ... dung beetles. They all have their part to play and depend on one another for survival.

Today humans all over the world are changing their habits to ensure that the planet can withstand our human demands. Africa is no different.
Visit the information centres at Letaba, Berg-en-dal and Skukuza to find out more.

Staff at these centres are trained to answer questions, so don't be shy to ask. They're only too pleased to share their knowledge.
In many rest camps, wildlife films are shown at night, so check the times and titles at the camp reception.

Malaria

The Eastern Transvaal Lowveld is a malaria area.

You should have started a course of anti-malaria tablets before arriving. If you have not been able to do this, tablets can be bought from a rest camp shop. Remember to follow the dosage instructions and continue taking the tablets after leaving the area.
In the summer months, especially at dusk and dawn, protect yourself by using an anti-mosquito repellent.

Squirrels stand rigid with anger and chatter very noisily when there is danger nearby, such as a snake or bird of prey.

Impala lily

Kruger is here for research

Serious, in-depth research is done constantly by Kruger scientists. Studies are in progress looking at the interrelated cycles of many types of life in the Park, from dragonflies to elephants. This information has many uses:

- ❑ It helps with the management of soil, vegetation and animal life within Kruger.
- ❑ It provides information for other conservation areas with fewer scientific resources.
- ❑ It provides vital information for farmers living nearby who have similar soil, weather and altitude to Kruger.
- ❑ Many research projects provide fascinating information about life in Kruger that add significantly to the visitor's enjoyment. One continuing project involves counting the populations of the larger mammals.

Animal census totals Kruger National Park 1980 – 1992

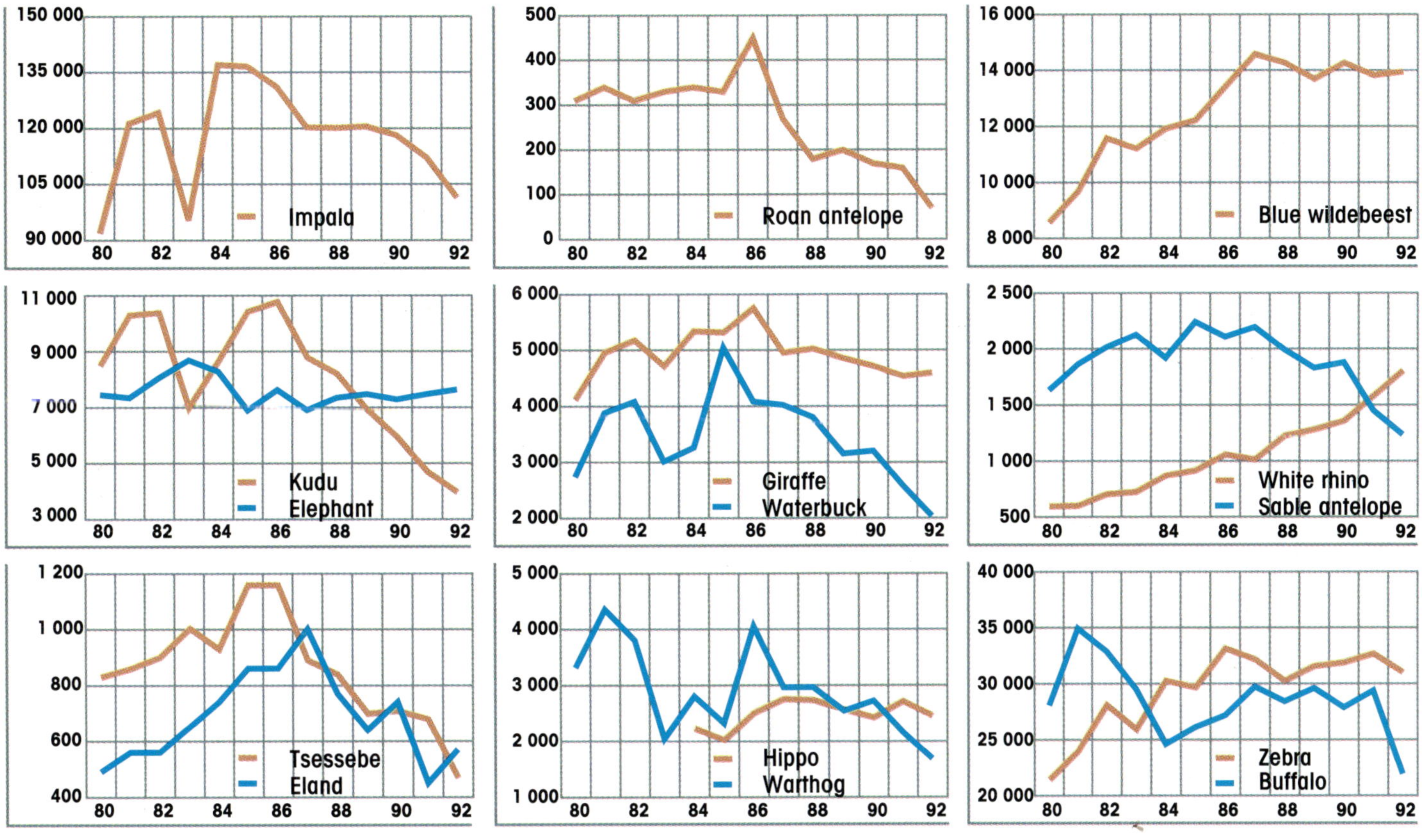

	1982	1983	1984	1992
Impala	124 280	95 420	137 060	101 420
Zebra	28 120	25 970	30 280	31 040
Buffalo	32 860	29 490	24 590	21 880
Blue wildebeest	11 590	11 220	11 930	13 960
Elephant	8 050	8 680	8 270	7 630
Giraffe	5 170	4 720	5 340	4 600
Kudu	10 390	7 000	8 860	3 970
Waterbuck	4 090	3 010	3 260	2 030
White rhino	700	730	870	1 800
Warthog	3 800	2 040	2 800	1 680
Sable antelope	2 010	2 130	1 920	1 230
Eland	580	650	740	570
Tsessebe	900	1 000	930	470
Roan antelope	310	330	340	70

The numbers of different animals change from year to year for many reasons.
The most important of these is rainfall, and therefore the availablity of food.
Each year KNP scientists do a count of the larger herbivores (plant-eating animals).
The table shows the impact of the 1982/83 drought and the recovery made by some of the affected herbivores by 1984. It also shows the effect of the recent drought in 1991/92.

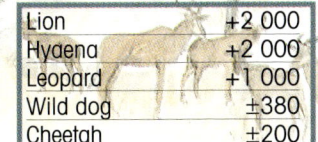

Lion	+2 000
Hyaena	+2 000
Leopard	+1 000
Wild dog	±380
Cheetah	±200

It is difficult to establish how many carnivores (meat-eating animals) there are in KNP. An estimate of the numbers of the major species is shown in the table.

Distance Grids

DISTANCES AND APPROXIMATE TIMES TAKEN BETWEEN GATES AND MAIN REST CAMPS

e.g. Berg-en-dal to Skukuza: distance = 72 km; approximate time = 2 hours 55 minutes (2h55)

DISTANCE: Kilometres
TIME: Hours & minutes

	Skukuza	Shingwedzi	Satara	Punda Maria	Pretoriuskop	Phalaborwa Gate	Paul Kruger Gate	Pafuri Gate	Orpen	Olifants	N'wanetsi	Numbi Gate	Mopani	Malelane	Lower Sabie	Letaba	Crocodile Bridge	Berg-en-dal
Berg-en-dal	72 / 2h55	344 / 13h45	165 / 6h35	415 / 16h35	92 / 3h40	285 / 11h25	83 / 3h20	453 / 18h10	213 / 8h30	219 / 8h45	180 / 7h10	97 / 3h50	281 / 11h15	12 / 0h30	113 / 4h30	234 / 9h25	149 / 6h00	•
Crocodile Bridge	77 / 3h05	306 / 12h15	127 / 5h05	377 / 15h05	125 / 5h00	246 / 9h50	88 / 3h30	415 / 16h35	175 / 7h00	181 / 7h15	142 / 5h40	130 / 5h10	243 / 9h45	141 / 5h40	34 / 1h20	196 / 7h50	•	149 / 6h00
Letaba	162 / 6h30	109 / 4h20	69 / 2h45	176 / 7h00	211 / 8h25	51 / 2h00	173 / 6h55	218 / 8h45	117 / 4h40	32 / 1h20	94 / 3h45	216 / 8h40	47 / 1h55	226 / 9h00	162 / 6h30	•	196 / 7h50	234 / 9h25
Lower Sabie	43 / 1h45	271 / 10h50	93 / 3h45	342 / 13h40	90 / 3h35	213 / 8h30	53 / 2h10	380 / 15h10	141 / 5h40	147 / 5h55	108 / 4h20	95 / 3h50	209 / 8h20	105 / 4h10	•	162 / 6h30	34 / 1h20	113 / 4h30
Malelane	64 / 2h35	333 / 13h20	156 / 6h15	408 / 16h20	85 / 3h25	277 / 11h05	74 / 3h00	444 / 17h45	204 / 8h10	210 / 8h25	170 / 6h50	94 / 3h50	272 / 10h55	•	105 / 4h10	226 / 9h00	141 / 5h40	12 / 0h30
Mopani	209 / 8h20	63 / 2h30	116 / 4h40	130 / 5h10	258 / 10h20	74 / 3h00	220 / 8h50	172 / 6h55	164 / 6h35	86 / 3h25	141 / 5h40	263 / 10h30	•	272 / 10h55	209 / 8h20	47 / 1h55	243 / 9h45	281 / 11h15
Numbi Gate	54 / 2h10	325 / 13h00	147 / 5h55	396 / 15h50	9 / 0h20	267 / 10h40	65 / 2h35	434 / 17h20	195 / 7h50	201 / 8h00	162 / 6h30	•	263 / 10h30	94 / 3h50	95 / 3h50	216 / 8h40	130 / 5h10	97 / 3h50
N'wanetsi	108 / 4h20	203 / 8h10	25 / 1h00	274 / 11h00	156 / 6h15	145 / 5h50	119 / 4h45	312 / 12h30	63 / 2h30	79 / 3h10	•	162 / 6h30	141 / 5h40	170 / 6h50	108 / 4h20	94 / 3h45	142 / 5h40	180 / 7h10
Olifants	147 / 5h55	141 / 5h40	54 / 2h10	212 / 8h30	195 / 7h50	83 / 3h20	158 / 6h20	250 / 10h00	102 / 4h05	•	79 / 3h10	201 / 8h00	86 / 3h25	210 / 8h25	147 / 5h55	32 / 1h20	181 / 7h15	219 / 8h45
Orpen	137 / 5h30	226 / 9h00	48 / 1h55	297 / 11h55	184 / 7h20	167 / 6h40	152 / 6h05	335 / 13h25	•	102 / 4h05	63 / 2h30	195 / 7h50	164 / 6h35	204 / 8h10	141 / 5h40	117 / 4h40	175 / 7h00	213 / 8h30
Pafuri Gate	380 / 15h10	109 / 4h20	287 / 11h30	76 / 3h00	438 / 17h30	246 / 9h50	392 / 15h40	•	335 / 13h25	250 / 10h00	312 / 12h30	434 / 17h20	172 / 6h55	444 / 17h45	380 / 15h10	218 / 8h45	415 / 16h35	453 / 18h10
Paul Kruger Gate	12 / 0h30	283 / 11h20	104 / 4h10	354 / 14h10	60 / 2h25	224 / 9h00	•	392 / 15h40	152 / 6h05	158 / 6h20	119 / 4h45	65 / 2h35	220 / 8h50	74 / 3h00	53 / 2h10	173 / 6h55	88 / 3h30	83 / 3h20
Phalaborwa Gate	213 / 8h30	137 / 5h30	119 / 4h45	201 / 8h00	261 / 10h25	•	224 / 9h00	246 / 9h50	167 / 6h40	83 / 3h20	145 / 5h50	267 / 10h40	74 / 3h00	277 / 11h05	213 / 8h30	51 / 2h00	246 / 9h50	285 / 11h25
Pretoriuskop	49 / 2h00	318 / 12h45	140 / 5h35	389 / 15h35	•	261 / 10h25	60 / 2h25	438 / 17h30	184 / 7h20	195 / 7h50	156 / 6h15	9 / 0h20	258 / 10h20	85 / 3h25	90 / 3h35	211 / 8h25	125 / 5h00	92 / 3h40
Punda Maria	342 / 13h40	71 / 2h50	245 / 9h50	•	389 / 15h35	201 / 8h00	354 / 14h10	76 / 3h00	297 / 11h55	212 / 8h30	274 / 11h00	396 / 15h50	130 / 5h10	408 / 16h20	342 / 13h40	176 / 7h00	377 / 15h05	415 / 16h35
Satara	93 / 3h45	178 / 7h10	•	245 / 9h50	140 / 5h35	119 / 4h45	104 / 4h10	287 / 11h30	48 / 1h55	54 / 2h10	25 / 1h00	147 / 5h55	116 / 4h40	156 / 6h15	93 / 3h45	69 / 2h45	127 / 5h05	165 / 6h35
Shingwedzi	271 / 10h50	•	178 / 7h10	71 / 2h50	318 / 12h45	137 / 5h30	283 / 11h20	109 / 4h20	226 / 9h00	141 / 5h40	203 / 8h10	325 / 13h00	63 / 2h30	333 / 13h20	271 / 10h50	109 / 4h20	306 / 12h15	344 / 13h45
Skukuza	•	271 / 10h50	93 / 3h45	342 / 13h40	49 / 2h00	213 / 8h30	12 / 0h30	380 / 15h10	137 / 5h30	147 / 5h55	108 / 4h20	54 / 2h10	209 / 8h20	64 / 2h35	43 / 1h45	162 / 6h30	77 / 3h05	72 / 2h55

Distances taken on shortest tarred routes. (N.B. Distances on sand roads may sometimes be shorter)

Time estimated travelling at 25 km/h

Be flexible

Life moves at a different speed in the Park. So must the drivers.

❑ Do not be too rigid about a planned route. As a rule of thumb, you should not expect to travel more than 25 km in an hour.

❑ Take plenty of food and drink in the car and let the relaxed mood of the bushveld be your guide.

❑ If you are changing rest camps, arriving or leaving, try not to travel more than 200 km in one day.

DISTANCES (kms) AND TIMES (hrs and mins) BETWEEN PRIVATE/BUSHVELD REST CAMPS AND NEARBY MAIN REST CAMPS

		DISTANCE	TIME
Bateleur	Mopani	65	2h35
	Shingwedzi	38	1h30
Biyamiti	Malelane	39	1h30
Boulders	Mopani	33	1h20
	Phalaborwa	54	2h10
Jakkalsbessie	Skukuza	5	0h10
Jock of the Bushveld	Malelane	33	1h20
	Skukuza	36	1h25
Roodewal	Olifants	30	1h10
	Satara	45	1h50
Shimuwini	Mopani	45	1h50
	Letaba	66	2h40
Sirheni	Punda Maria	54	2h10
	Shingwedzi	35	1h25
Talamati	Orpen	30	1h10
	Satara	52	2h05

Leopard tortoises take 15 years to mature sexually. The female is, apparently, a reluctant sexual partner, and only gives in after being pursued and bumped by her mate.

Visitor Facilities at Get-out Points and Gates

VISITOR FACILITIES

	Toilets	Shade	Seating	Braai area	Boiling water	Cooking gas	Cool drinks only	Shoplets/kiosk	Hot refreshments	Wood for sale	Telephone	Educational display
GET-OUT POINTS 🚗												
Afsaal ☕	●	●	●	●	●	●		●	●	●	●	
Albasini Ruins												●
Babalala	●	●	●	●	●	●					●	
Bird Hide (Shingwedzi)		●	●									●
Bird Hide (Skukuza)		●	●									
Bobbejaan Krans												
Hippo Pool												
Kruger Tablets												
Masorini	●	●	●	●	●	●	●				●	
Mlondozi Dam	●	●	●		●	●	●			●		
Mooi Plaas	●	●	●		●	●	●			●		
Muzandzeni	●	●	●		●	●	●					
Nhlanguleni	●	●	●		●	●	●					
Nkuhlu ☕	●	●	●	●				●	●	●		
Nkumbe	●	●	●									
N'wamanzi												
N'wanetsi	●	●	●	●		●					●	
Orpen Dam	●	●	●									
Pafuri Picnic	●	●	●									
Rabelais' Hut												●
Stevenson-Hamilton												
Timbavati	●	●	●	●	●							
Tshanga	●	●										
Tshokwane ☕	●	●	●	●		●		●	●	●	●	
GATES 📫												
Crocodile Bridge	●	●	●	●		●		●		●	●	
Malelane	●	●	●			●						
Numbi	●	●	●									
Orpen	●	●	●	●	●	●		●				
Pafuri	●					●						
Paul Kruger	●										●	
Phalaborwa	●	●	●									
Punda Maria	●										●	
☕ Main picnic place												

GET-OUT POINTS & GATES

🚶🚗 **Get-out Points**
- ❏ You may get out of your car at these places!
- ❏ See **Visitor Facilities** grid on this page and **Maps** on pages 24-35

Monkey business

Of the many mammals in the Park, baboons and monkeys are the most comfortable near humans. Feeding them is dangerous for you, but even more dangerous for them. Their normal eating behaviour is disturbed and they no longer rely on the bushveld for their food, demanding to be fed by people. Once they become a threat to humans, they have to be shot by Park rangers.

🚗 **Look-out Points**
- ❏ You may **not** get out of your car at these places
- ❏ No facilities.
- ❏ Good for game-watching or general views.
- ❏ See **Maps** on pages 24-35 for these Look-out Points

Monkeys groom one another as a form of socialising and communicating with other members of the troop.

Visitor Facilities at Rest Camps

VISITOR FACILITIES	Day visitor facilities*	Camping and caravan	Conference facilities	Swimming pool (residents only)	In camp trail	Environmental educ. centre	Educational display	Petrol station	Car wash	AA Emergency services	Car hire	Airport	Shop	Restaurant/cafetaria	Bank	Post office	Telephone	Doctor	Laundromat
MAIN																			
Berg-en-dal	•	•	•	•	•	•	•	•					•	•			•		•
Crocodile Bridge	•	•						•					•	•			•		•
Letaba	•	•			•	•	•	•		•			•	•			•		•
Lower Sabie		•						•					•	•			•		•
Mopani		•		•	•	•							•	•			•		•
Olifants	•						•	•					•	•			•		•
Orpen	•							•									•		•
Pretoriuskop	•	•		•	•								•	•			•		•
Punda Maria	•	•			•								•	•			•		•
Satara	•	•					•	•		•			•	•			•		•
Shingwedzi	•	•		•			•	•					•	•			•		•
Skukuza	•	•			•	•	•	•	•	•	•	•	•	•	•	•	•	•	•
OTHER																			
Private																			
Boulders																			
Jock of the Bushveld						•													
Malelane																			
N'wanetsi																			
Roodewal																			
Bushveld																			
Bateleur			•														•		
Biyamiti																	•		
Jakkalsbessie			•														•		
Shimuwini																	•		
Sirheni																	•		
Talamati																	•		
Camping																			
Balule		•																	
Maroela		•																	
Tamboti (Tent Camp)																			

Day visitor facilities include toilets, shade, seating and braai area

REST CAMPS

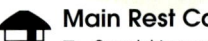

Main Rest Camps
- ❏ Overnight accommodation & facilities for day visitors.
- ❏ See **Visitor Facilities grid** on this page and *Maps* on pages 24-35.

Other Rest Camps
- ❏ Private, Bushveld, Camping
- ❏ No day visitor facilities.
- ❏ No entry without booking.
- ❏ See **Visitor Facilities grid** on this page and *Maps* on pages 24-35.

Travel slowly and you'll see more ... safely

The roads in Kruger are not only for motorists.
Animals and birds often use them to move around more easily.
So travel slowly and avoid scaring away any wildlife close to the road.
Speeding can result in a collision with game – which is tragic for the animal and may also damage your car.

Be courteous to others as you drive

There is no telling what may lie around the next bend and you certainly don't want to scare anything away. When you see a car ahead of you that has stopped, approach very slowly and quietly.

Trail Base Camps
- ❏ Walking trails.
- ❏ No day visitor facilities.
- ❏ No entry without booking.
- ❏ See *Maps* on pages 24-35.

Rest camp life

Day-time

The rest camp offers you some special opportunities.

- ❏ Trees are difficult to learn in the bushveld … but easy in camp where they have labels with names and numbers to help you.
- ❏ You will be amazed at the abundant birdlife, in the lush vegetation, in the rest camps.
- ❏ In rest camps along the rivers, look into the large trees for bats and monkeys. You'll also see lizards, squirrels, beetles and butterflies.

Night-time

Many different and exciting animals come out at night! Listen for their noises and look for them with a torch along the rest camp fences.

- ❏ Look at the dozens of incredible insects that are attracted to your torch.
- ❏ Walk along the fences and see what 'eyes' light up in the bushveld … bushbuck, impala, civet, genet and maybe even hippo. Nightjars lie still on patches of warm, bare sand and their eyes shine red in your torch light. Hyaena and jackal come to smell the meat on the braai … but do not offer them even a scrap.
- ❏ Turn off your torch and use binoculars to experience the brilliant stars – with no pollution masking their sparkle.
- ❏ Above all, listen! There are nightjars, owls and dikkops. And you'll hear the roars, yelps and cackles of the nocturnal predators … lion, jackal and hyaena.

Noisy birds, like grey louries, puffbacks and forktailed drongos, give raucous alarm calls. They often dive-bomb owls, such as the pearl-spotted owl, which roost in large shady trees during the day.

Look out for trees with numbers to help you identify them. This is a sausage tree – number 678.

Certain species of animals and birds learn to scavenge more readily than others. Hornbills and starlings are often seen at rest camps and picnic sites.

Kruger Park Regulations and Gate Times

Times for Entry gates and Camp gates

	Jan	Feb	Mar	Apr	May-July	August	Sept	Oct	Nov-Dec
Open	04:30 (camp gate) 05:30 (entry gate)	05:30	05:30	06:00	06:00	06:00	06:00	05:30	04:30 (camp gate) 05:30 (entry gate)
Close	18:30	18:30	18:00	18:00	17:30	18:00	18:00	18:00	18:30

Opening and closing times

❑ **Reception**
 Open: 08:00 Close: 17:30

❑ **Shops**
 Open: 08:00
 Close: ½ hour after
 gates close

❑ **Accommodation**
 Can be occupied from 12:00
 on arrival day. Must be
 vacated before 09:00
 on departure day.

❑ **Restaurants**
 Breakfast: 07:00 – 09:00
 Lunch: 12:00 – 14:00
 Dinner: 18:00 – 21:00

Park Regulations

Kruger has a few necessary regulations. These are essential to ensure the safety and protection of the visitors, as well as the animal and plant life.
You must obey all of them. Thoughtless people who break them will be fined.

❑ Drive on approved roads only; do not drive on unmarked roads at any time.
❑ The speed limit is 50 km/h on tarred roads and 40 km/h on untarred roads ... and there are speed traps to catch speedsters.
❑ Only a person with a valid licence may drive a vehicle.
❑ Unless you are at an area marked on the **Map**, you must stay in your car at all times.

Camp Regulations

❑ Do not cause a disturbance at any time.
❑ There must be no noise between 21:30 and 06:00.
❑ The use of roller skates, skateboards and bicycles is forbidden.
❑ You may not advertise or trade.
❑ The speed limit within rest camps is 10 km/h.
❑ No pets are allowed.
❑ Firearms must be declared.

Environmental Conservation

❑ Littering is prohibited. Put all your litter into a rubbish bin, and be sure to close the lid properly.
❑ Feeding of the animals is prohibited. This includes in the camp and by the fences.
❑ No animal, bird, plant or object may be disturbed or removed.
❑ Do not upset or frighten any animal.
❑ Be aware of the danger of fire when handling burning objects (braai wood, coals, cigarettes etc.).
❑ Do not waste water or electricity.

Further Information

❑ For Visitor Facilities, see pages 15-16.
❑ For further information, ask at the camp reception.

Emergencies (Fire or Medical)

❑ During the day, go to the reception.
❑ During the night, drive to the camp gate and hoot.

Kruger Booking

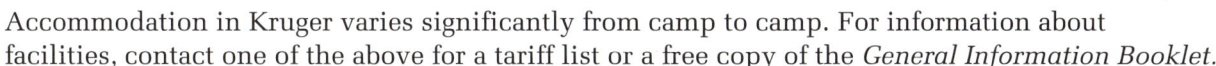

Kruger accommodation is very popular during school holidays and over weekends. Trails are popular throughout the year and are closed during the December/January school holidays. To have the best opportunity of obtaining a booking of your choice you should apply **in writing 13 months** in advance. e.g. for December 1995, apply before the end of December 1994.

There are often cancellations. So give our booking offices a ring :

Pretoria	Tel : (012) 343-1991	Fax : (012) 343-0905
Cape Town	Tel : (021) 22-2810	Fax : (021) 24-6211

Accommodation in Kruger varies significantly from camp to camp. For information about facilities, contact one of the above for a tariff list or a free copy of the *General Information Booklet.*

Make a photostat copy of this booking slip and send it to:

National Parks Board P. O. Box 787, Pretoria, 0001
P. O. Box 7400, Rogge Bay, 8012

Application for accommodation/trails

Surname and initials ....

Postal address ....

....

.... Postal code ....

ID .... Fax ( ) ....

Telephone H ( ) .... W ( ) ....

No of persons: Adults 16 years and older ☐   Children under 16 years of age at time of intended visit ☐   Babies under 2 years of age at time of intended visit ☐

SA citizens (or persons with a permanent residential permit) - 65 years and older, may qualify for a discount. Contact the booking office for discount details. Please give relevant names and ID's.

Surname and initials .... ID ....

Reservation required (please indicate with X)

Trail: Name of trail.. Date of commencement..............................

Camping: Caravan ☐   Tent ☐   Furnished tent ☐

Accommodation: Cottage ☐   Hut ☐ (with bathroom/shower)   Hut ☐ (with communal ablution)

Specify any other requirements ....

Itinerary

Restcamps	Date of arrival	No. of nights	Departure date	No. of units/sites

Any other information for the attention of the reservation officer:

....

....

Signature.. Date..

Fish eagles mate for life. They dive in a spectacular way to catch fish, but are also scavengers. Listen for their unique ringing call.

What can you do at home?

Find out more about how to use your rubbish in a responsible way. We cannot afford to throw everything away together in one bag. This is throwing away resources. Have two separate rubbish bins in your kitchen:

- ❏ Use one rubbish bin for degradable matter, such as vegetable peelings and eggshells. These make great compost in the same way that the falling leaves and decomposing animal dung fertilise the soil in the Park.

- ❏ Use the other bin for non-degradable items, such as glass bottles, newspapers, plastic and tin. These can be separated and taken to recycling centres near your home.

Rubbish in Kruger is now sorted in this manner at rest camp dumps. In the old days these areas were an eyesore and an unnatural attraction for baboons and hyaena.

Hippos usually spend the heat of the summer days in water. They graze on grasses at night

As a protection mechanism, chameleons change colour rapidly, according to the colour of their habitat. They hiss aggressively if you get too close.

Committed to serving Nature.

Grewia

KRUGER NATIONAL PARK MAP

Kruger National Park Map

These areas have been enlarged on pages 24-35

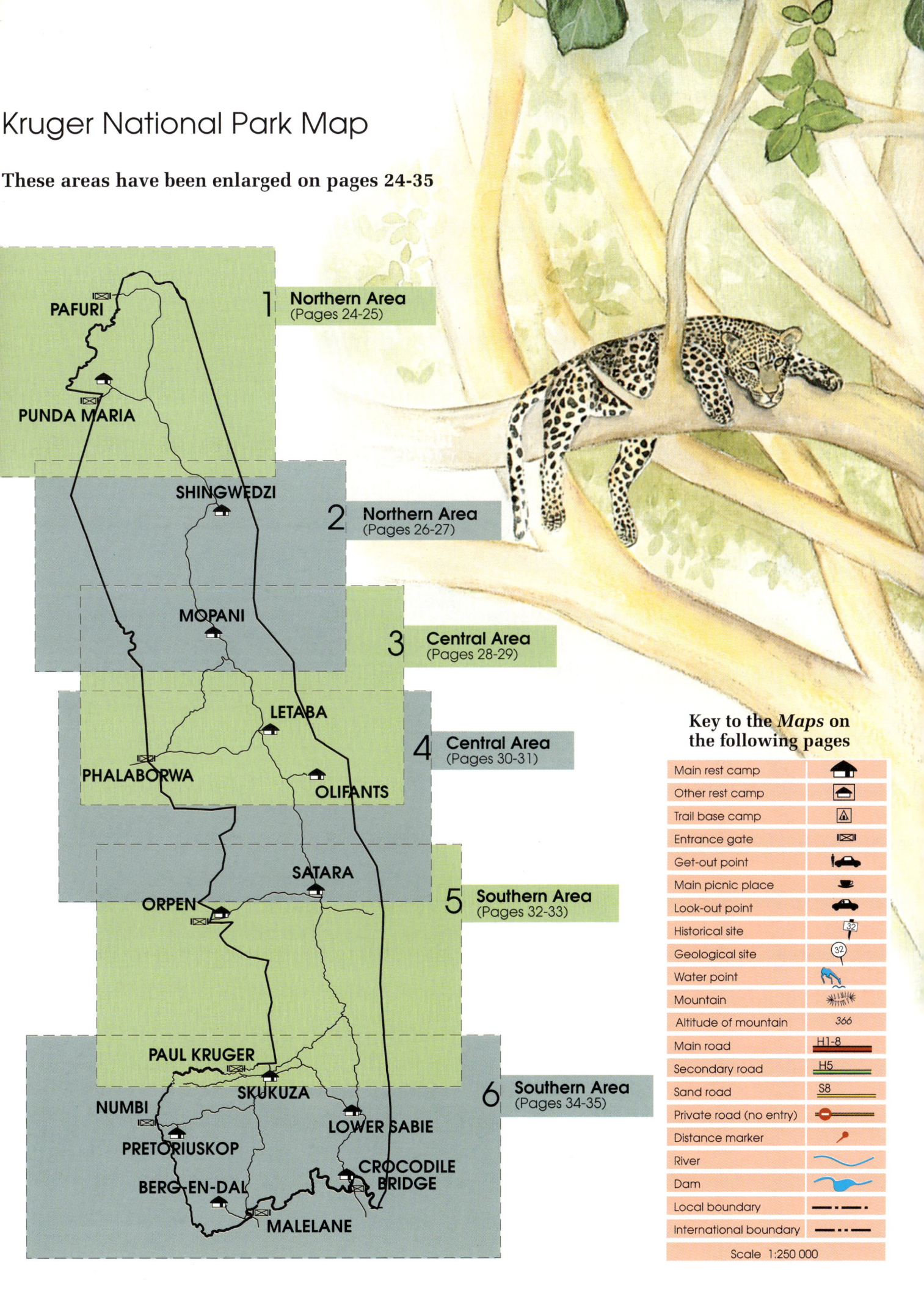

1 Northern Area
(Pages 24-25)

2 Northern Area
(Pages 26-27)

3 Central Area
(Pages 28-29)

4 Central Area
(Pages 30-31)

5 Southern Area
(Pages 32-33)

6 Southern Area
(Pages 34-35)

PAFURI

PUNDA MARIA

SHINGWEDZI

MOPANI

LETABA

PHALABORWA

OLIFANTS

SATARA

ORPEN

PAUL KRUGER

NUMBI

SKUKUZA

PRETORIUSKOP

LOWER SABIE

BERG-EN-DAL

CROCODILE BRIDGE

MALELANE

Key to the *Maps* on the following pages

Main rest camp	
Other rest camp	
Trail base camp	
Entrance gate	
Get-out point	
Main picnic place	
Look-out point	
Historical site	32
Geological site	32
Water point	
Mountain	
Altitude of mountain	*366*
Main road	H1-8
Secondary road	H5
Sand road	S8
Private road (no entry)	
Distance marker	
River	
Dam	
Local boundary	
International boundary	
Scale 1:250 000	

23

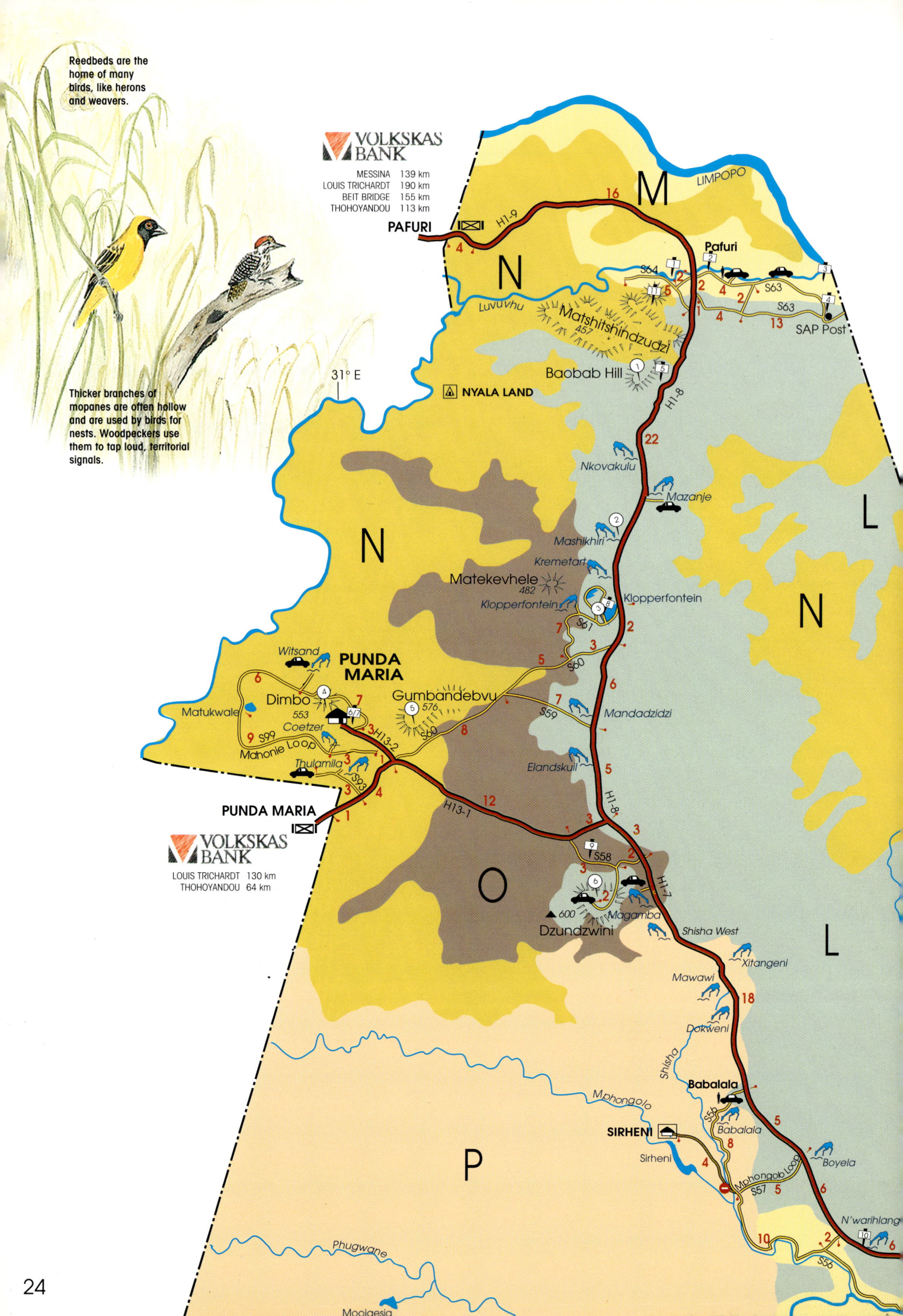

Reedbeds are the home of many birds, like herons and weavers.

Thicker branches of mopanes are often hollow and are used by birds for nests. Woodpeckers use them to tap loud, territorial signals.

PAFURI

M

N

Pafuri

LIMPOPO

H1-9

16

4

S64

2

2

4

2

S63

11

5

2

1

4

S63

13

SAP Post

Luvuvhu

Matshitshindzudzi
457

Baobab Hill

1

5

H1-8

▲ NYALA LAND

22

N

L

Nkovakulu

Mazanje

Mashikhiri

2

Kremetart

Matekevhele
482

Klopperfontein

3

8

Klopperfontein

N

S61

7

2

S60

3

5

6

Witsand

PUNDA MARIA

6

Dimbo
553

4

7

6/7

Gumbandebvu
576

5

7

S59

Mandadzidzi

Matukwale

Coetzer

3

H13-2

S60

8

Elandskuil

5

9

S99

Mahonie Loop

Thulamila

S93

3

4

H13-1

12

H1-8

5

3

3

3

H1-7

PUNDA MARIA

1

9

S58

2

O

6

2

▲ 600

Dzundzwini

Magamba

Shisha West

Xitangeni

Mawawi

18

Dokweni

L

Babalala

Shisha

S56

Babalala

5

SIRHENI

Mphongolo

8

Boyela

Sirheni

4

Mphongob Loop

6

P

S57

5

10

N'warihlang

2

10

6

S56

Phugwane

Mooigesig

31° E

Your place in the Park

❑ We are no less, nor greater than the animals or the plants.

❑ We are visitors to a unique type of environment that now exists in only a few places on Earth. As we are lucky enough to share in Kruger's wonders, we must respect it and keep it natural. It is inexcusable to leave litter anywhere — here in Kruger, or at home. Litter is not only very ugly, but also causes sickness and harm, and can be fatal to those living nearby.

Litter is life-threatening!

❑ If herbivores eat plastic, they can die of starvation because their digestive systems fail.

❑ Birds can choke to death or can lose a limb if they get tangled in string.

❑ If animals stand on a piece of broken glass or sharp tin, infection can set in and they can lose their ability to feed or protect themselves.

❑ If they are trapped by something someone has left behind, they could die of starvation.

These problems are not only costly in terms of animal life, but in the end affect your own pocket. For the Park to remain clean and undisturbed as it should be, all rubbish has to be collected and disposed of. This costs money.
Be proud of your Park. It is a priceless collection of life.
Littering here – or at home – destroys the environment for everyone.

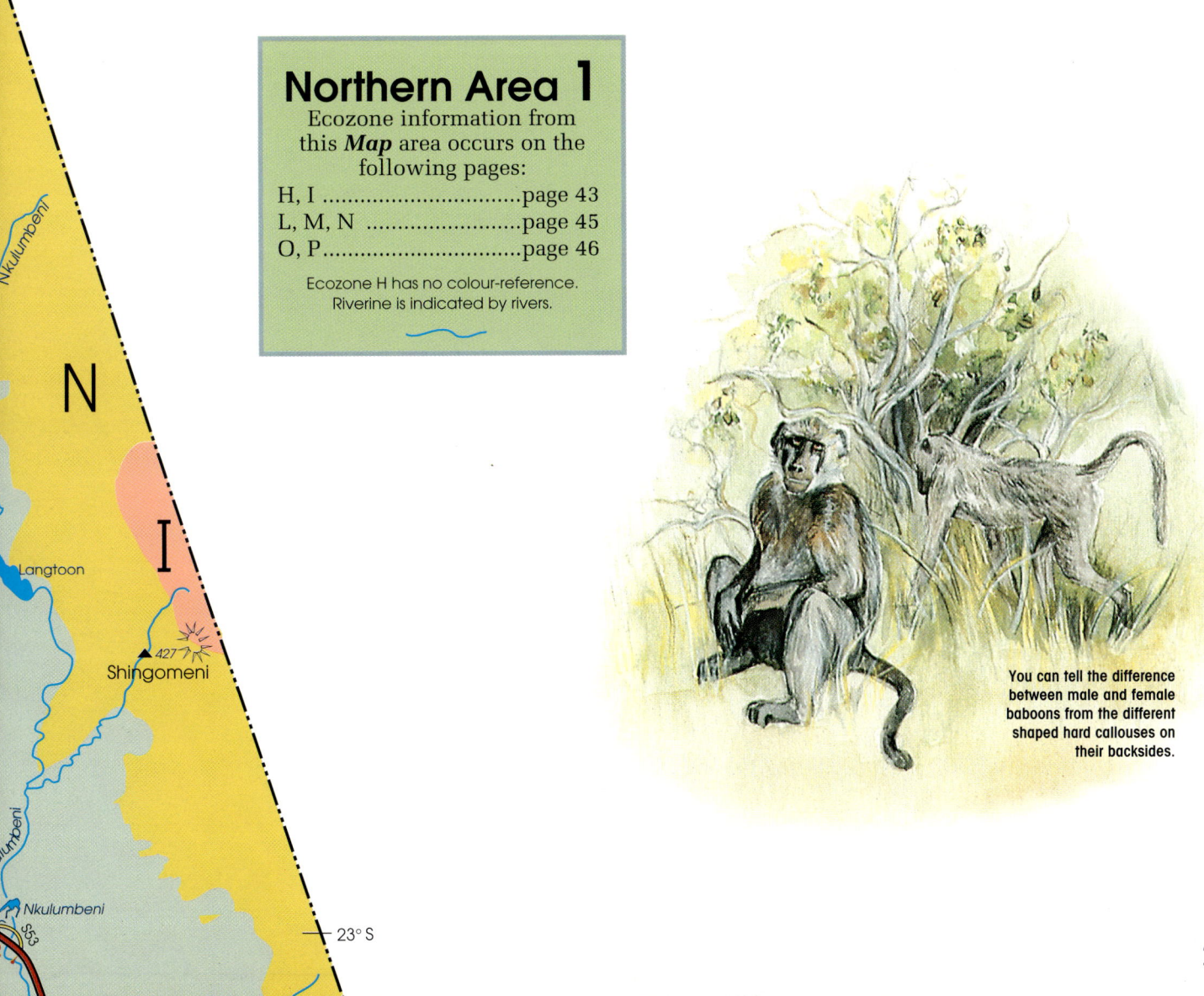

Northern Area 1
Ecozone information from this *Map* area occurs on the following pages:

H, I ....page 43
L, M, N ....page 45
O, P..............................page 46

Ecozone H has no colour-reference.
Riverine is indicated by rivers.

Langtoon

N

I

▲427
Shingomeni

Nkulumbeni

Nkulumbeni

23° S

You can tell the difference between male and female baboons from the different shaped hard callouses on their backsides.

Successful spotting

*Whenever you stop, switch off
your engine.*

Listen ... and smell ... the uniqueness
of the bushveld.
Particularly when other cars are
nearby, it is important not to disturb
the natural surroundings with the
noise and fumes of a running
engine, a roaring air conditioner
or a loud radio.
A rustle in the grass, the excited
alarm call of a bird, the snap of a
twig, each indicate the whereabouts
of an animal or some activity that
you might have missed.
Listen carefully to the noises of nature.
You will learn to interpret the mating
calls, a mother calling her young and
even the alarm calls of bird or buck that
give away the presence of a
camouflaged leopard.

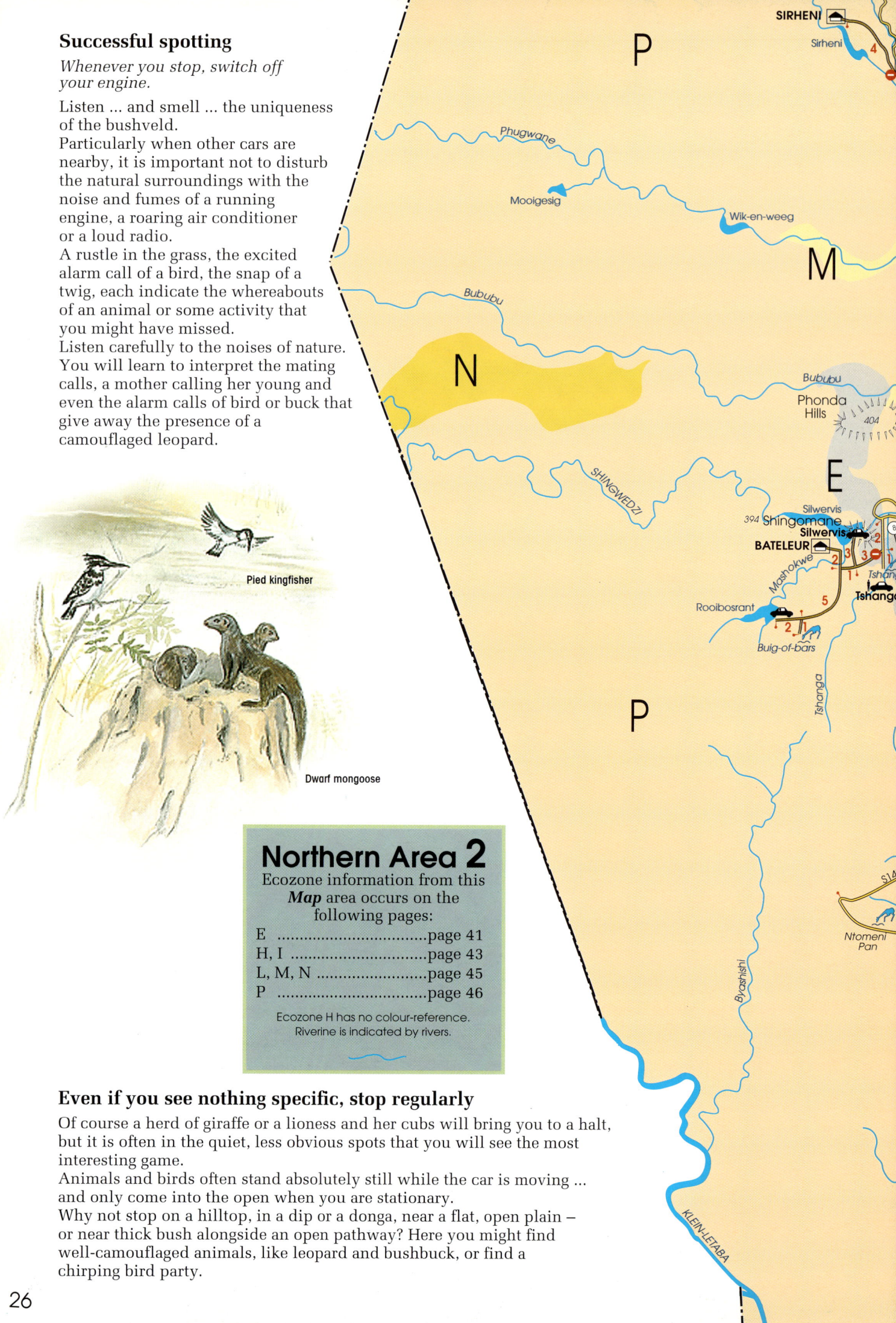

Pied kingfisher

Dwarf mongoose

Northern Area 2

Ecozone information from this
Map area occurs on the
following pages:

Ecozone H has no colour-reference.
Riverine is indicated by rivers.

Even if you see nothing specific, stop regularly

Of course a herd of giraffe or a lioness and her cubs will bring you to a halt,
but it is often in the quiet, less obvious spots that you will see the most
interesting game.
Animals and birds often stand absolutely still while the car is moving ...
and only come into the open when you are stationary.
Why not stop on a hilltop, in a dip or a donga, near a flat, open plain —
or near thick bush alongside an open pathway? Here you might find
well-camouflaged animals, like leopard and bushbuck, or find a
chirping bird party.

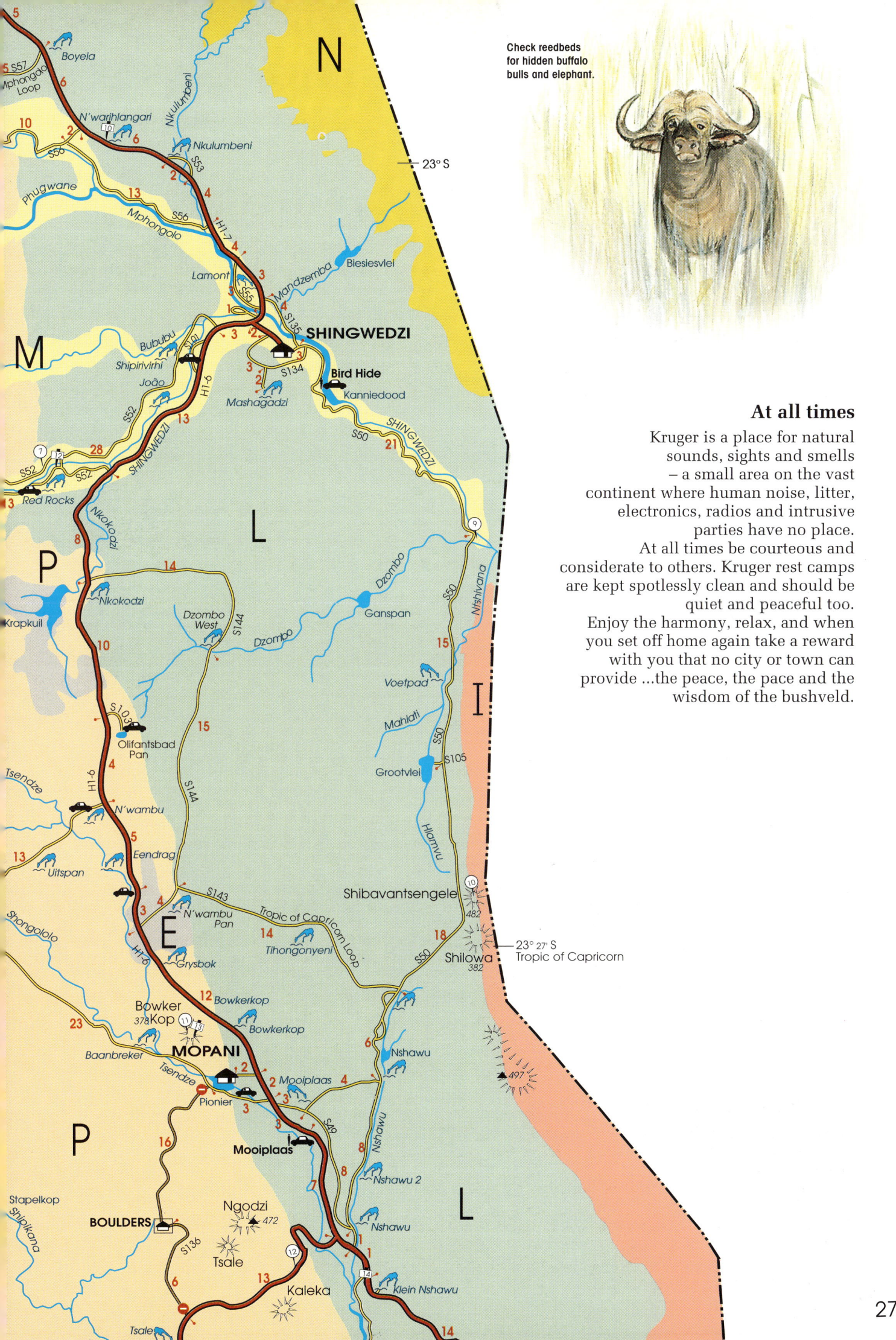

Check reedbeds for hidden buffalo bulls and elephant.

At all times

Kruger is a place for natural sounds, sights and smells – a small area on the vast continent where human noise, litter, electronics, radios and intrusive parties have no place.

At all times be courteous and considerate to others. Kruger rest camps are kept spotlessly clean and should be quiet and peaceful too.

Enjoy the harmony, relax, and when you set off home again take a reward with you that no city or town can provide ...the peace, the pace and the wisdom of the bushveld.

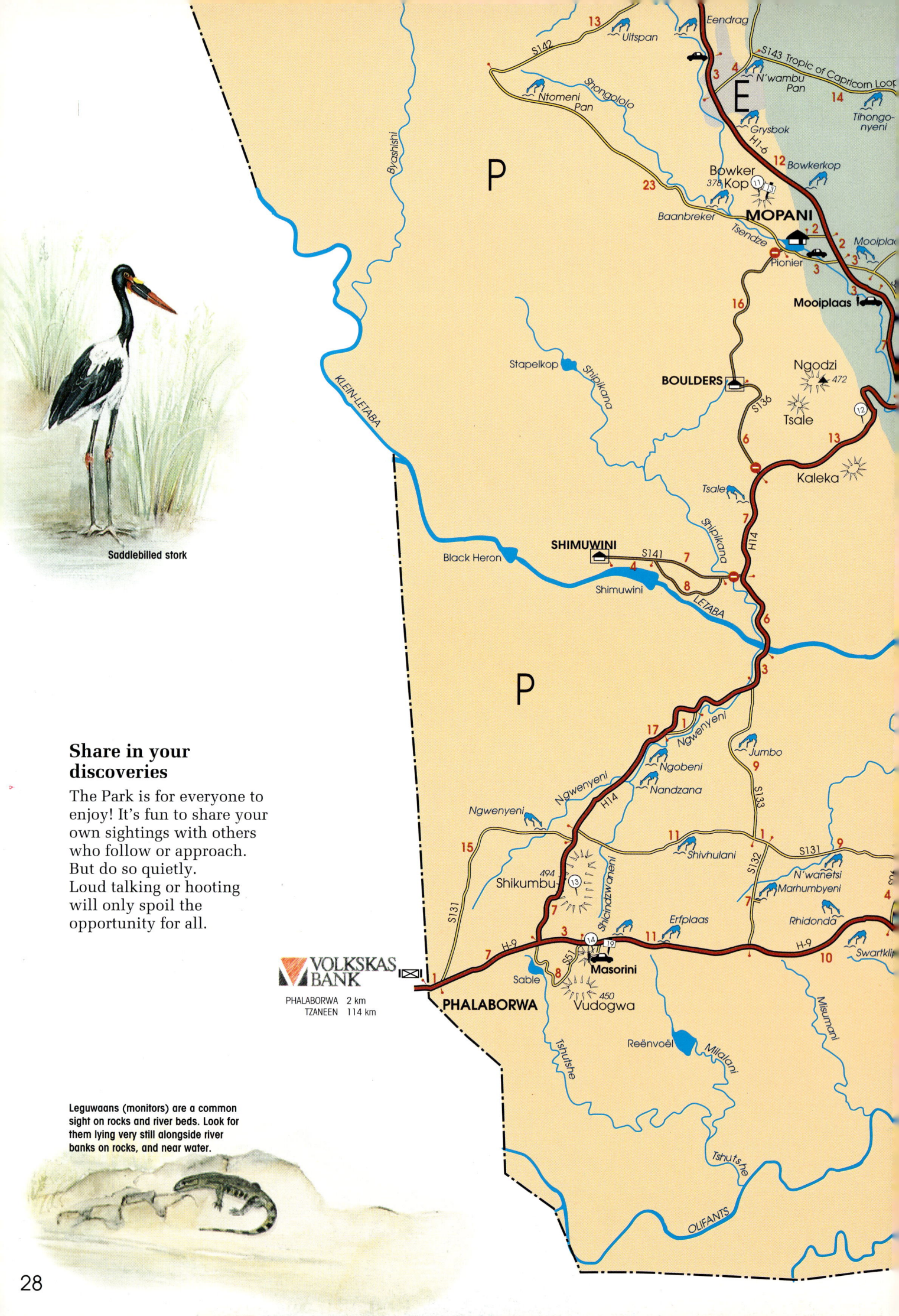

Saddlebilled stork

Share in your discoveries

The Park is for everyone to enjoy! It's fun to share your own sightings with others who follow or approach. But do so quietly. Loud talking or hooting will only spoil the opportunity for all.

Leguwaans (monitors) are a common sight on rocks and river beds. Look for them lying very still alongside river banks on rocks, and near water.

VOLKSKAS BANK

PHALABORWA 2 km
TZANEEN 114 km

Uitspan

S142

Ntomeni Pan

Shongololo

Byashishi

P

Eendrag

S143 Tropic of Capricorn Loop

E

N'wambu Pan

Tihongo-nyeni

14

13

Grysbok

H1-6

Bowker Kop

378

Bowkerkop

12

23

11

13

MOPANI

Baanbreker

Tsendze

2

Mooiplaas

3

Pionier

3

Mooiplaas

16

3

Stapelkop

Shipikana

BOULDERS

S136

Ngodzi

472

6

Tsale

13

Kaleka

KLEIN-LETABA

Tsale

7

H14

12

Black Heron

SHIMUWINI

S141

Shipikana

4

7

Shimuwini

8

LETABA

6

3

P

17

1

Ngwenyeni

Jumbo

Ngobeni

9

Ngwenyeni

Nandzana

S133

Ngwenyeni

15

11

Shivhulani

S131

S132

9

N'wanetsi

Shikumbu

494

13

Marhumbyeni

4

Shindzwaneni

7

Erfplaas

Rhidonda

S131

H-9

7

3

11

10

Swartklip

7

Masorini

8

S51

14

H-9

Sable

Misumari

450

PHALABORWA

Vudogwa

Tshutshe

Reênvoël

Milalani

Tshutshe

OLIFANTS

28

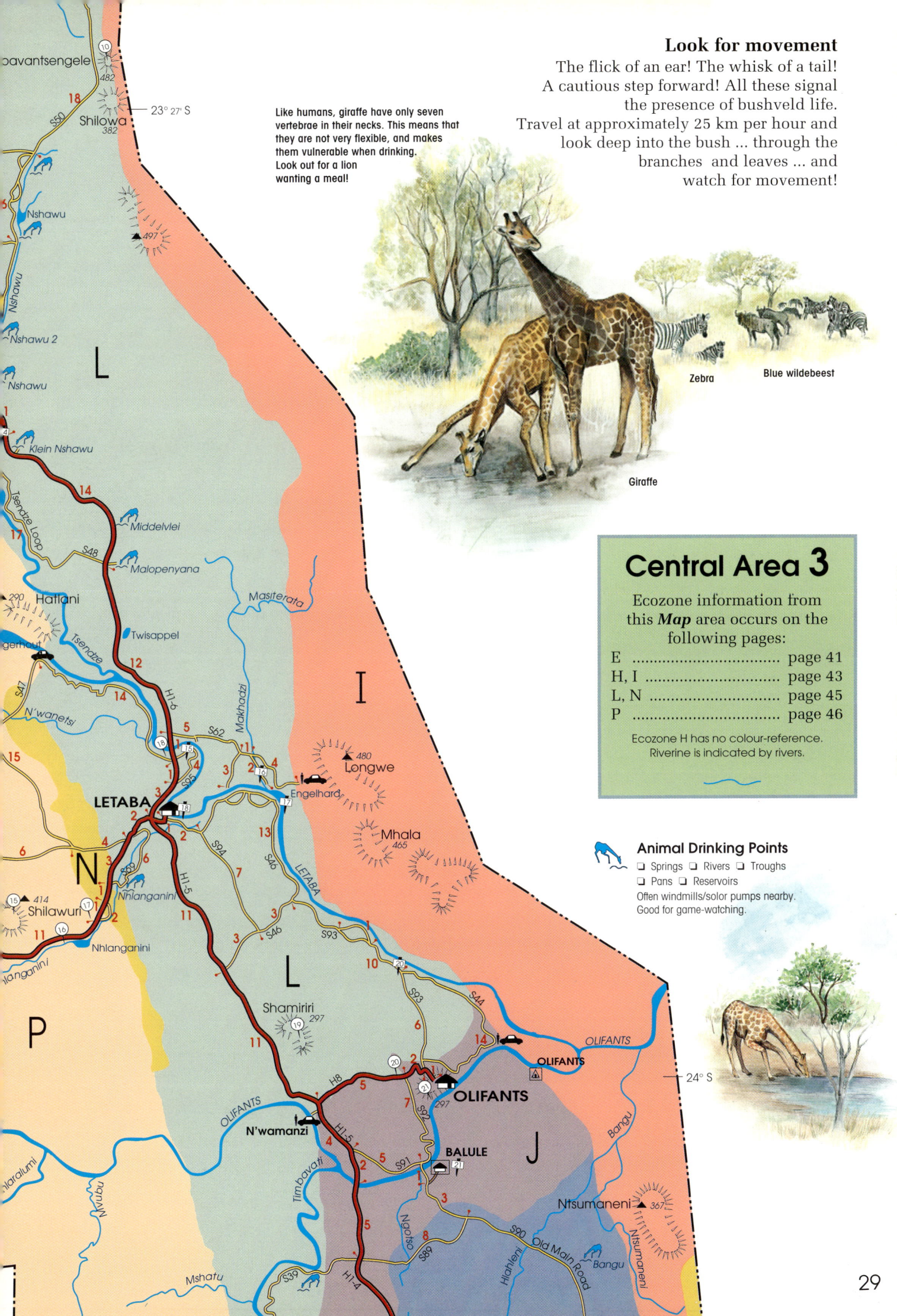

Look for movement

The flick of an ear! The whisk of a tail!
A cautious step forward! All these signal
the presence of bushveld life.
Travel at approximately 25 km per hour and
look deep into the bush ... through the
branches and leaves ... and
watch for movement!

Like humans, giraffe have only seven
vertebrae in their necks. This means that
they are not very flexible, and makes
them vulnerable when drinking.
Look out for a lion
wanting a meal!

Zebra

Blue wildebeest

Giraffe

Central Area 3

Ecozone information from
this *Map* area occurs on the
following pages:

E .... page 41
H, I .... page 43
L, N .... page 45
P .... page 46

Ecozone H has no colour-reference.
Riverine is indicated by rivers.

Animal Drinking Points

❏ Springs ❏ Rivers ❏ Troughs
❏ Pans ❏ Reservoirs
Often windmills/solor pumps nearby.
Good for game-watching.

bavantsengele

Shilowa

— 23° 27' S

Nshawu

Nshawu 2

Nshawu

Klein Nshawu

Middelvlei

Malopenyana

Masiterata

Hatlani

Twisappel

gerhout

N'wanetsi

Longwe

LETABA

Engelhard

Mhala

Nhlanganini

Shilawuri

Nhlanganini

Nhlanganini

Shamiriri

OLIFANTS

N'wamanzi

OLIFANTS

OLIFANTS

BALULE

Bangu

Ntsumaneni

Bangu

Ntsumaneni

Hlahleni

Old Main Road

Mshatu

— 24° S

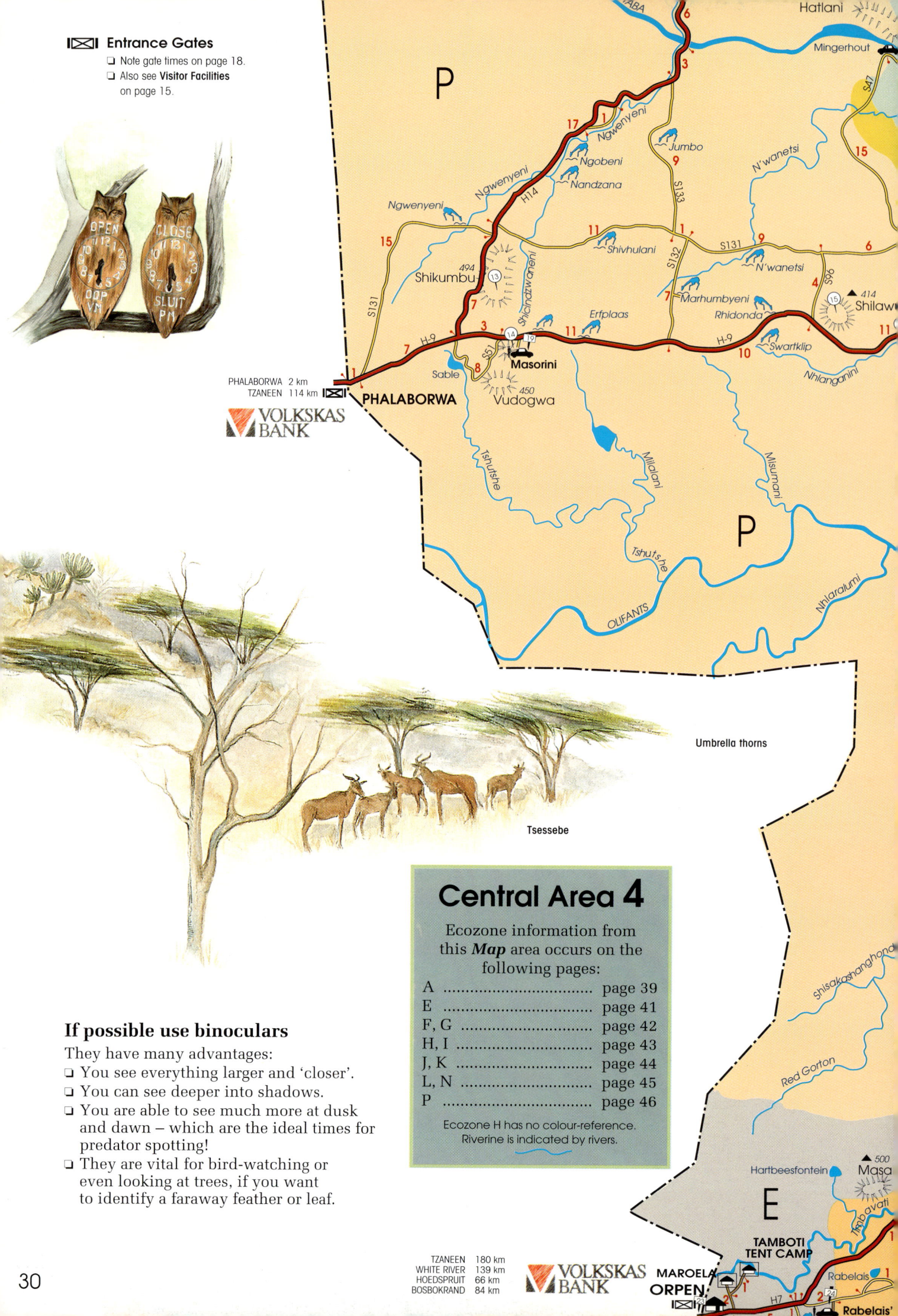

Entrance Gates
- ❏ Note gate times on page 18.
- ❏ Also see **Visitor Facilities** on page 15.

If possible use binoculars

They have many advantages:
- ❏ You see everything larger and 'closer'.
- ❏ You can see deeper into shadows.
- ❏ You are able to see much more at dusk and dawn – which are the ideal times for predator spotting!
- ❏ They are vital for bird-watching or even looking at trees, if you want to identify a faraway feather or leaf.

OPEN
OOP VM

CLOSE
SLUIT PM

P

Hatlani

Mingerhout

SA7

17

Ngwenyeni

Jumbo

N'wanetsi

15

Ngobeni

Nandzana

9

S133

15

Ngwenyeni

Ngwenyeni

H14

11

Shivhulani

S132

S131

9

6

Shikumbu

494

13

Erfplaas

11

Marhumbyeni

N'wanetsi

S96

S131

7

Shidziwaneni

H-9

3

14

19

11

Rhidonda

15

414

Shilaw

7

H-9

Masorini

10

Swartklip

11

S51

8

Sable

Vudogwa

450

Nhlanganini

PHALABORWA 2 km
TZANEEN 114 km

PHALABORWA

VOLKSKAS BANK

Tshutshe

Mlialani

Misumani

P

Tshutshe

Nhlaralumi

OLIFANTS

Umbrella thorns

Shisakashanghond

Tsessebe

Red Gorton

Central Area **4**

Ecozone information from this *Map* area occurs on the following pages:

Ecozone H has no colour-reference.
Riverine is indicated by rivers.

Masa

500

Hartbeesfontein

Timbavati

E

TAMBOTI TENT CAMP

Rabelais

TZANEEN   180 km
WHITE RIVER   139 km
HOEDSPRUIT   66 km
BOSBOKRAND   84 km

VOLKSKAS BANK

MAROELA

ORPEN

H7

Rabelais'

24

30

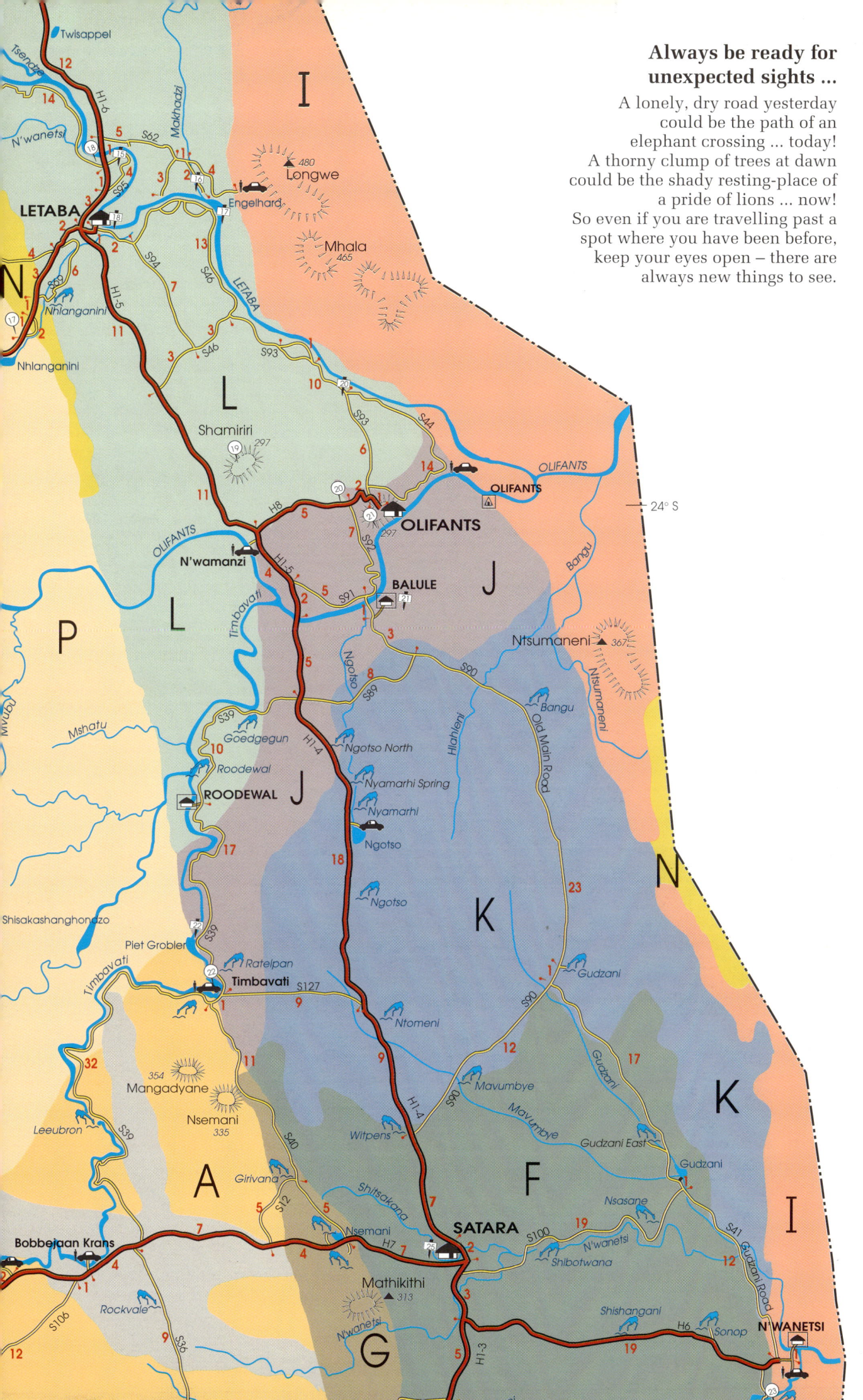

Always be ready for unexpected sights ...

A lonely, dry road yesterday could be the path of an elephant crossing ... today! A thorny clump of trees at dawn could be the shady resting-place of a pride of lions ... now! So even if you are travelling past a spot where you have been before, keep your eyes open – there are always new things to see.

24° S

31

The bushveld is waiting for you …

Camouflage is of vital importance to many animals for survival.
When they're standing still, their colour and shape blend in perfectly with their surroundings. Even if you drive past slowly, you need to look very carefully to find them.

TZANEEN 180 km
WHITE RIVER 139 km
HOEDSPRUIT 66 km
BOSBOKRAND 84 km

VOLKSKAS BANK

Warthog often eat roots and tubers – bending down on their knees, which allows them to dig with greater force.

Holes dug by antbears, with their sharp claws, are used many times over. After the antbear moves out, warthog, porcupine, python, mongoose, pangolin, wild dog, wild cat – and even hyaena and leopard – gradually dig bigger tunnels and use the space as a burrow, hide or warren.

Bobbejaan stert

Southern Area 5

Ecozone information from this *Map* area occurs on the following pages:

A .... page 39
B .... page 40
D, E .... page 41
F, G .... page 42
H, I .... page 43

Ecozone H has no colour-reference.
Riverine is indicated by rivers.

Koppies
❑ Hilly outcrops that rise above the general landscape.
❑ The Find it section has information on geology and what to look for in rocky areas (see pages 48 -51).

③² Geological Sites
❑ Interesting rock or landscape formation.
❑ See pages 48-51 for details of what to look for and where.

HAZYVIEW 42 km
SABIE 86 km
WHITE RIVER 84 km
BOSBOKRAND 87 km

VOLKSKAS BANK

Map labels: Red Gorton, Nsemani 335, Leeubron, S39, Girivana, P, A, Hartbeesfontein, Masala ▲500, Bobbejaan Krans, Timbavati, Rockvale, S106, S36, E, TAMBOTI TENT CAMP, MAROELA ORPEN, Rabelais, Rabelais' Hut, N'wamatsatsa, S140, A, Muzandzeni, S126, Sweni, Shimangwaneni, S145, TALAMATI, N'waswitsontso, Fairfield, Mondzweni, Mahlabyanini, Ngwenyeni, Ngwenyeni, S36, Nhlanguleni, Lugmag, S36, Mutlumuvi, E, Maroela Loop, Airport, JAKKALSBESSIE, Nursery, S41, Bird Hide, SAND H12, PAUL KRUGER, SABIE, S3, Doispane Road, Nyamundwa, Albasini Ruins, S104, S1, N'waswitshaka, SKUKUZA, H11, H4-1, B, D

32

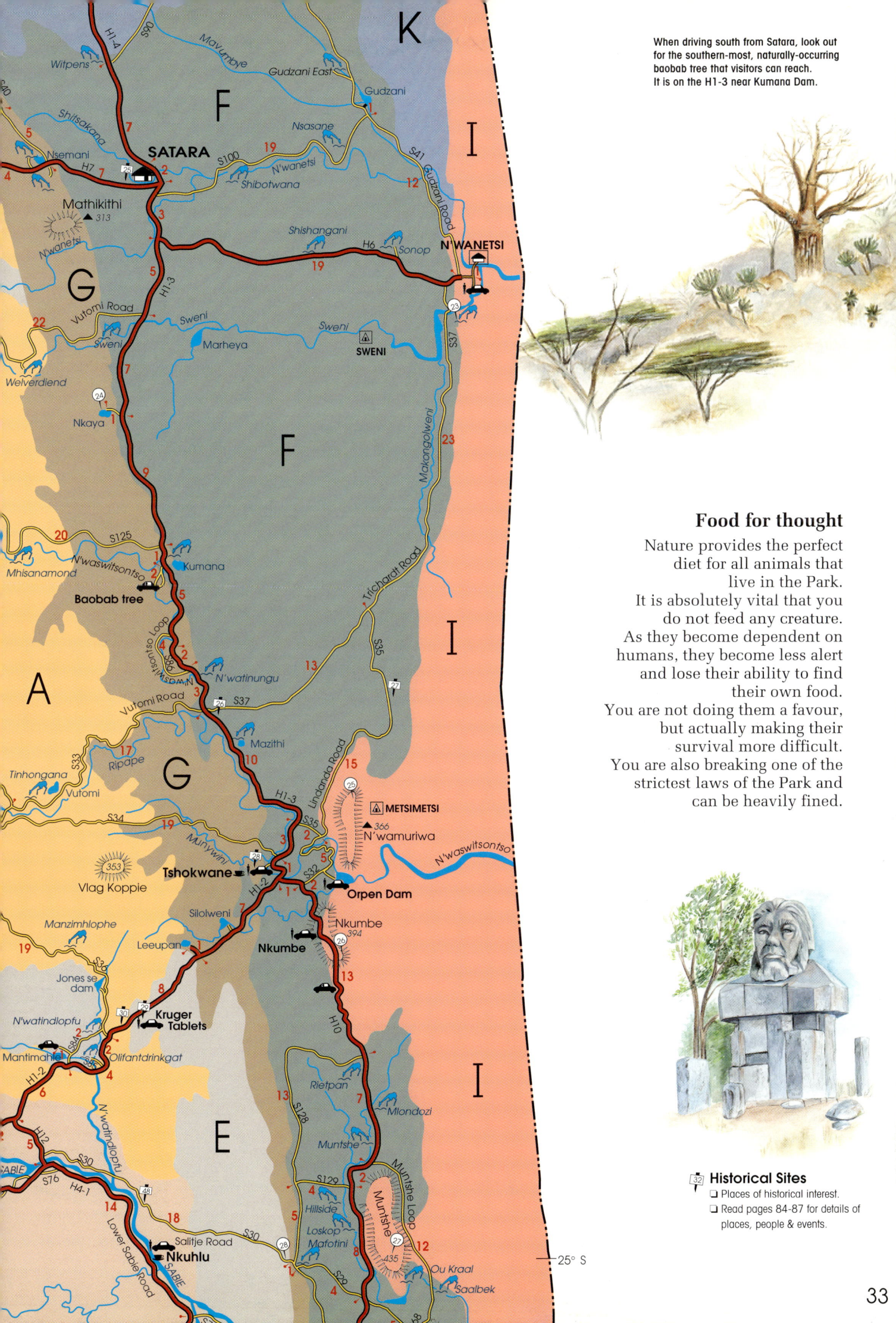

When driving south from Satara, look out for the southern-most, naturally-occurring baobab tree that visitors can reach. It is on the H1-3 near Kumana Dam.

Food for thought

Nature provides the perfect diet for all animals that live in the Park. It is absolutely vital that you do not feed any creature. As they become dependent on humans, they become less alert and lose their ability to find their own food. You are not doing them a favour, but actually making their survival more difficult. You are also breaking one of the strictest laws of the Park and can be heavily fined.

Historical Sites
❏ Places of historical interest.
❏ Read pages 84-87 for details of places, people & events.

33

Vultures in the trees are often waiting for their turn at the kill.

White-backed vulture

Vultures circling upwards in the sky are catching warm thermal air currents.

Vultures on the ground are usually feeding. Also be on the lookout for jackal, hyaena, lion and cheetah.

VOLKSKAS BANK

HAZYVIEW 42 km
SABIE 86 km
WHITE RIVER 84 km
BOSBOKRAND 87 km

VOLKSKAS BANK

HAZYVIEW 19 km
WHITE RIVER 32 km
NELSPRUIT 51 km

VOLKSKAS BANK

MALELANE 13 km
BARBERTON 84 km
NELSPRUIT 62 km
KANYAMAZANE 48 km

PAUL KRUGER
Airport
JAKKALSBESSIE
Nursery
Bird Hide
SKUKUZA

ALBASINI RUINS
Nyamundwa
Dolspane Road
Matlhari 451
Matupa 504
Mlaleni 492
N'waswitshaka
De Laporte
Mathekenyane 385
Stevenson-Hamilton
Shirimantanga 450
Renosterkoppies (Shirimantanga)

Mtshawu
Mestel
Shabeni 759
Napi Road
Napi 505
Shiphampanane
Kwaggaspan
Siyalu 341

NUMBI
Pretorius Kop 732
Manungu 689
PRETORIUSKOP
Shitlhave
Biyamiti
NAPI
Muhlambamadvube
Bume Road

Ship Mountain 662
Voortrekker Road
Komapiti
Josékhulu
Voortrekker
JOCK OF THE BUSHVELD
Makhutlwanini 418
Biyamiti Weir
Biyamiti

Sitfungwane 691
Newu 666
Mitomeni
Afsaal
Jock
Biyamiti Loop

Mangake 697
Newu
Mlambane
Ampie se Boorgat
James

Stolsnek
Renosterpan
Mlambane Loop

WOLHUTER
Matjulu 627
Timfenheni Loop

BOESMAN
Matjulu
Matjulu Loop
Matjulu

Maqili 674
BERG-EN-DAL
Tlhalabye 630
MALELANE

Khandzalive 839
MALELANE

CROCODILE

31° 30' E

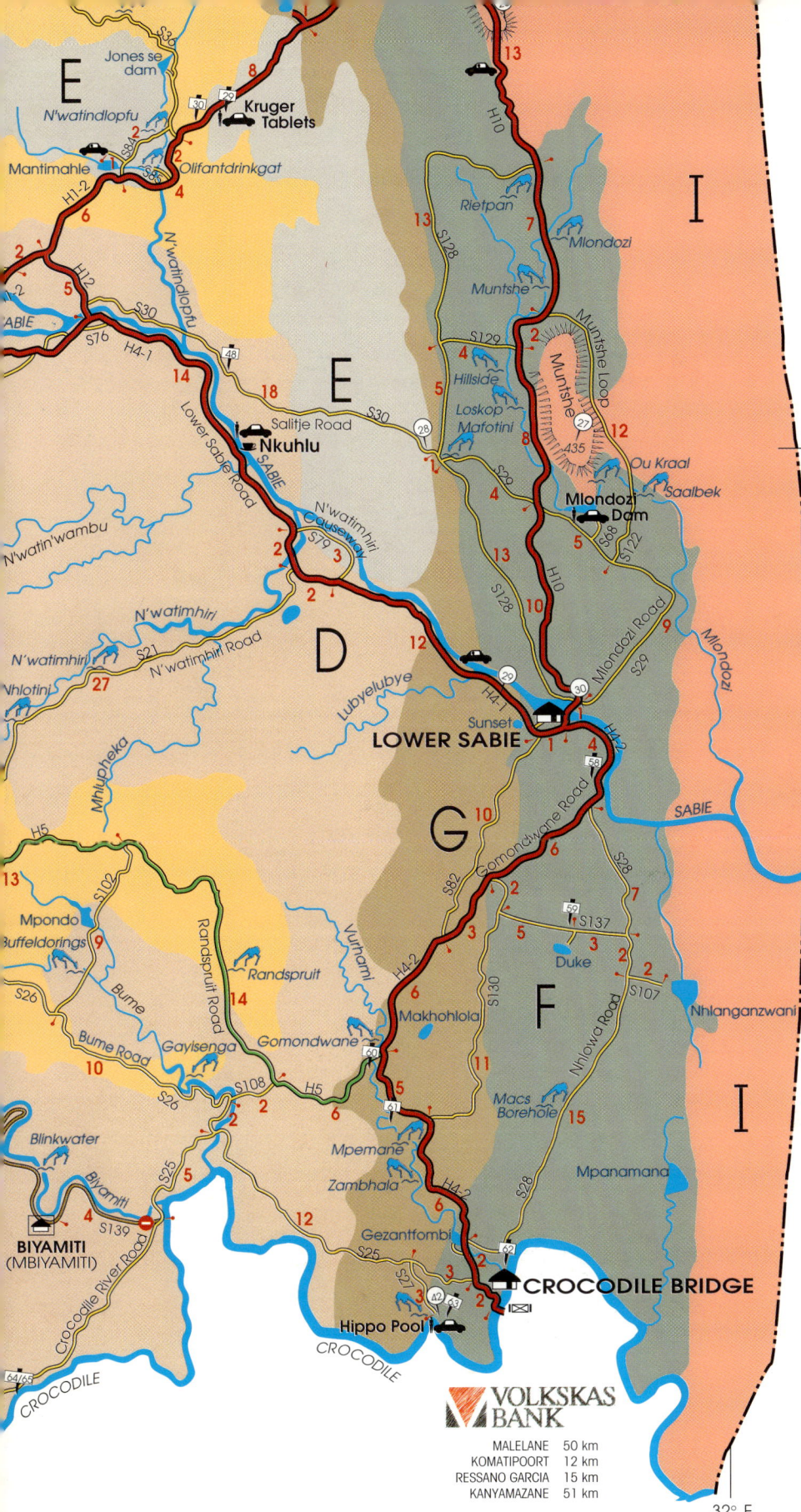

❑ The best times for game-viewing are early morning and late afternoon. As the day heats up, animals move into the deep shade and tend to stand completely still or lie down.

❑ The hotter midday period is the ideal time for you to relax near a waterhole, where there is always something of interest. The shade alongside a dry river-bed or at a rest camp also provides relaxation and plenty to entertain you.

❑ Watching birds or identifying trees are ideal pastimes when game is scarce for any reason. Kruger has over 500 species of birds, over 300 different trees and over 200 larger visible mammals. Kruger visitors have plenty to keep them interested ... wherever they are ... whatever the season or time of day!

25° S

32° E

VOLKSKAS BANK

MALELANE   50 km
KOMATIPOORT   12 km
RESSANO GARCIA 15 km
KANYAMAZANE   51 km

Southern Area 6

Ecozone H has no colour-reference.
Riverine is indicated by rivers.

A touchy subject

Everything in the Park has a purpose, and is part of the chain of life. A twig may be home to a beetle. A bundle of straw may be the nest of a bird. To drive over, touch or take anything away will fundamentally disturb the balance of nature.
It is crucial that you leave even the smallest things alone – like sticks, stones, horns, bones and seed pods.
Your souvenir could be the end of a small animal's life.

Take the excitement of Kruger home with you!

Many of the plants, insects, birds, and even a few of the smaller animals, can be seen in towns and on farms throughout South Africa. If you take time to look, if you sense the quietness and power of the Park, you will slowly come to understand it. It will become part of you. Wherever you live, the cycle of life – between soil, water, plants, insects and animals – is fascinating. What you learn here in Kruger is often happening on your own doorstep!

Insectivorous birds, such as forktailed drongos, stay close to antelope herds. They eat the insects which move as the antelope pass through the grass and undergrowth.

Young impala males, under a year old, have short, straight horns (penkoppe), while the two-year-old males have horns that curl inwards (knypkoppe).

Swainson's francolin

Commitment to our clients.
It's in our nature.

36

ECOZONES

General Ecozone Information

The Kruger National Park **Map** (see pages 24-35) has been divided by the scientists working in the Park into 16 natural areas or Ecozones. Each Ecozone has been given a name, a specific colour and a letter, from A to P (e.g. A is Mixed Bushwillow Woodlands).

Ecozones have their own distinct combination of geology, land-shape and rainfall which gives rise to different patterns of vegetation and associated animals.

By studying the diagrams illustrating each Ecozone you will be able to interpret Kruger through new eyes because you will be able to look for animals and plants in the right habitat.

Using the Ecozone information will enable you to add to the interest and excitement of your stay in Kruger.

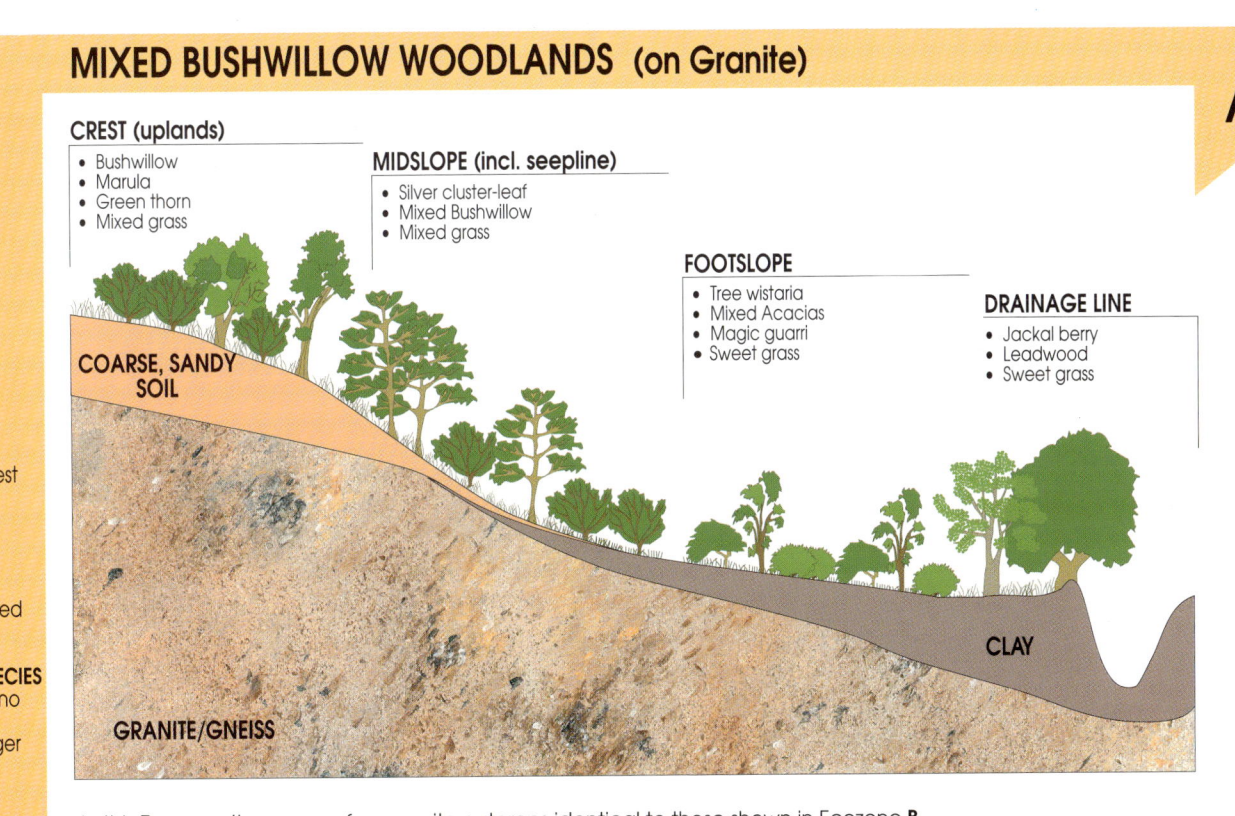

MIXED BUSHWILLOW WOODLANDS (on Granite)

A

CREST (uplands)
- Bushwillow
- Marula
- Green thorn
- Mixed grass

MIDSLOPE (incl. seepline)
- Silver cluster-leaf
- Mixed Bushwillow
- Mixed grass

FOOTSLOPE
- Tree wistaria
- Mixed Acacias
- Magic guarri
- Sweet grass

DRAINAGE LINE
- Jackal berry
- Leadwood
- Sweet grass

COARSE, SANDY SOIL

GRANITE/GNEISS

CLAY

LOOK FOR

BROWSERS
- Giraffe
- Kudu
- Impala
- Duiker

GRAZERS
- Wildebeest
- Zebra

PREDATORS
- Lion
- Hyaena
- Side-striped jackal

SPECIAL SPECIES
- White rhino
- Sable
- Klipspringer

In this Ecozone there are a few granite outcrops identical to those shown in Ecozone **B**.

Ecozone A occurs in the following *Map* areas:
Central Area 4   – Pages 30-31
Southern Area 5 – Pages 32-33
Southern Area 6 – Pages 34-35

PRETORIUSKOP SOURVELD (on Granite)

B

LOOK FOR

BROWSERS
• Giraffe
• Kudu
• Impala
• Duiker

GRAZERS
• Reedbuck

PREDATORS
• Wild dog
• Lion
• Side-striped jackal

SPECIAL SPECIES
• White rhino
• Sable
• Mountain reedbuck
• Klipspringer

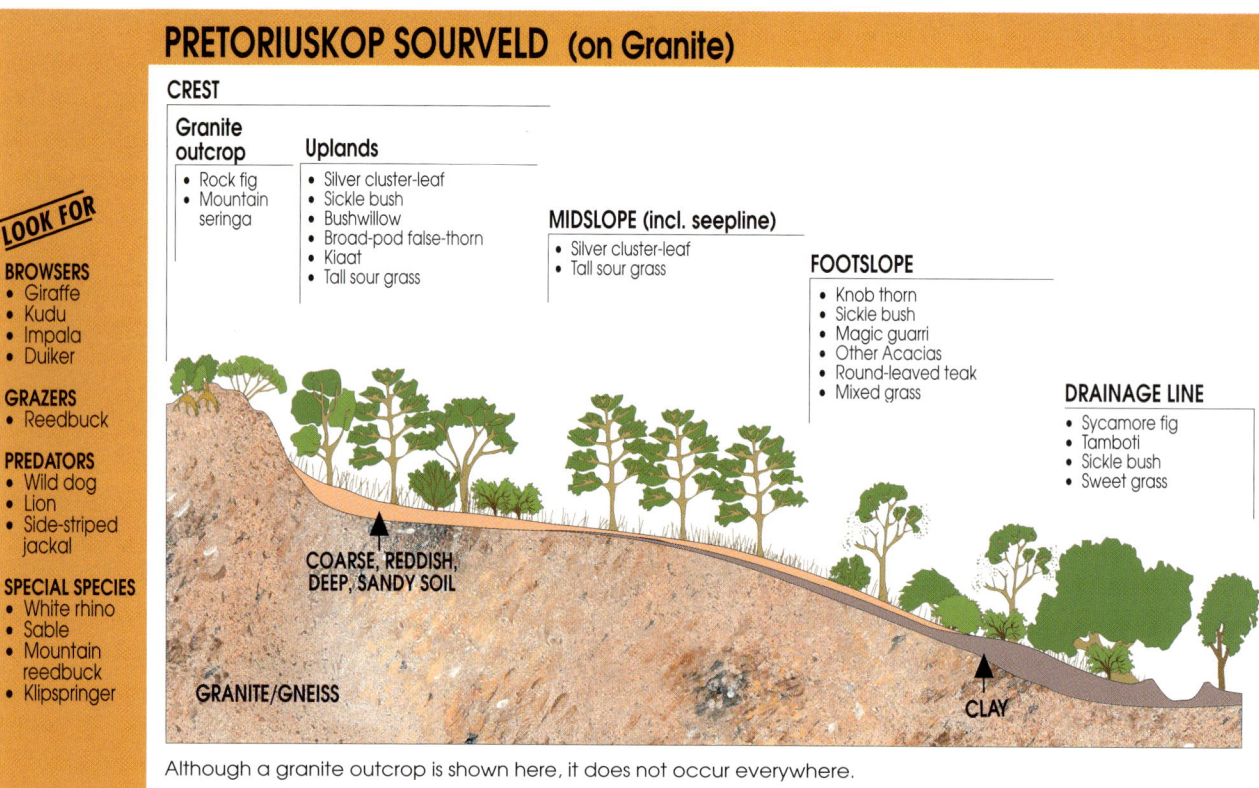

CREST

Granite outcrop
• Rock fig
• Mountain seringa

Uplands
• Silver cluster-leaf
• Sickle bush
• Bushwillow
• Broad-pod false-thorn
• Kiaat
• Tall sour grass

MIDSLOPE (incl. seepline)
• Silver cluster-leaf
• Tall sour grass

FOOTSLOPE
• Knob thorn
• Sickle bush
• Magic guarri
• Other Acacias
• Round-leaved teak
• Mixed grass

DRAINAGE LINE
• Sycamore fig
• Tamboti
• Sickle bush
• Sweet grass

COARSE, REDDISH, DEEP, SANDY SOIL

GRANITE/GNEISS

CLAY

Although a granite outcrop is shown here, it does not occur everywhere.

Ecozone B occurs in the following *Map* areas:
Southern Area 5 – Pages 32-33
Southern Area 6 – Pages 34-35

MALELANE MOUNTAIN BUSHVELD (on Granite)

C

LOOK FOR

BROWSERS
• Impala
• Kudu

GRAZERS
• Waterbuck
• Reedbuck

PREDATORS
• Wild dog
• Hyaena

SPECIAL SPECIES
• White rhino
• Sable
• Mountain reedbuck
• Klipspringer

CREST

Rocky outcrop
• Rock fig
• Mountain seringa

Uplands
• Bushwillow
• Sour grass

MIDSLOPE
• Bushwillow
• Mixed grass

FOOTSLOPE
• Magic guarri
• Impala lily
• Sweet grass

DRAINAGE LINE
• Jackal berry
• Tamboti
• Wild date palm
• Sweet grass

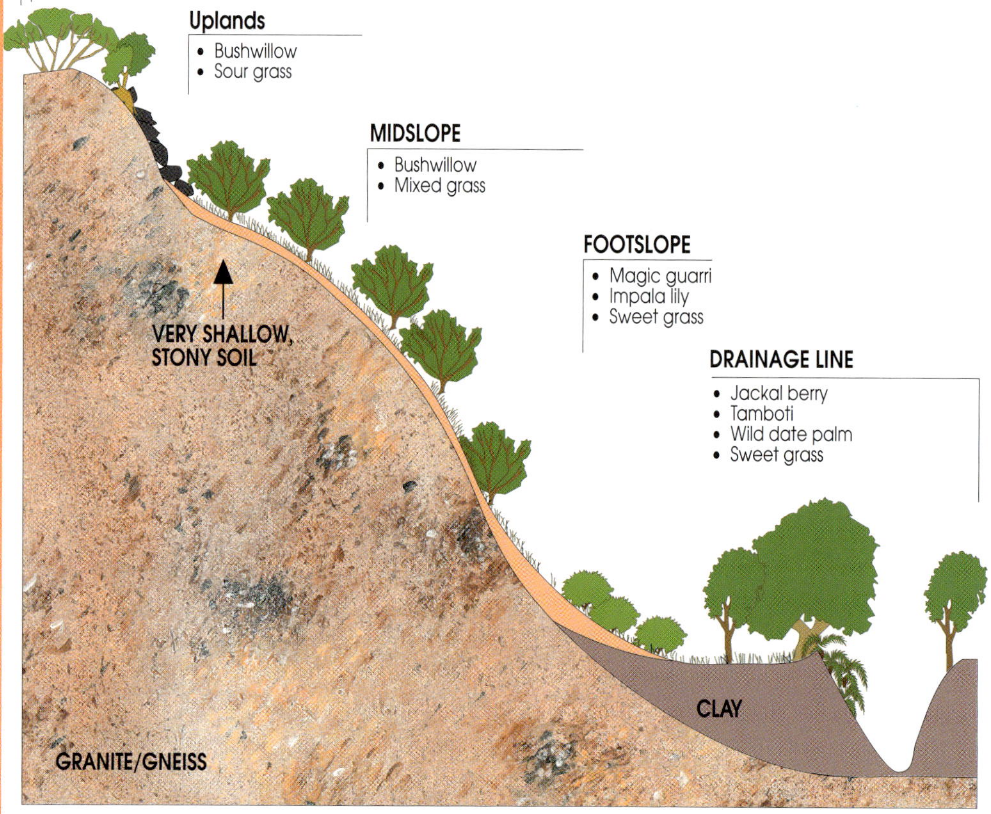

VERY SHALLOW, STONY SOIL

GRANITE/GNEISS

CLAY

Ecozone C occurs in the following *Map* areas:
Southern Area 6 – Pages 34-35

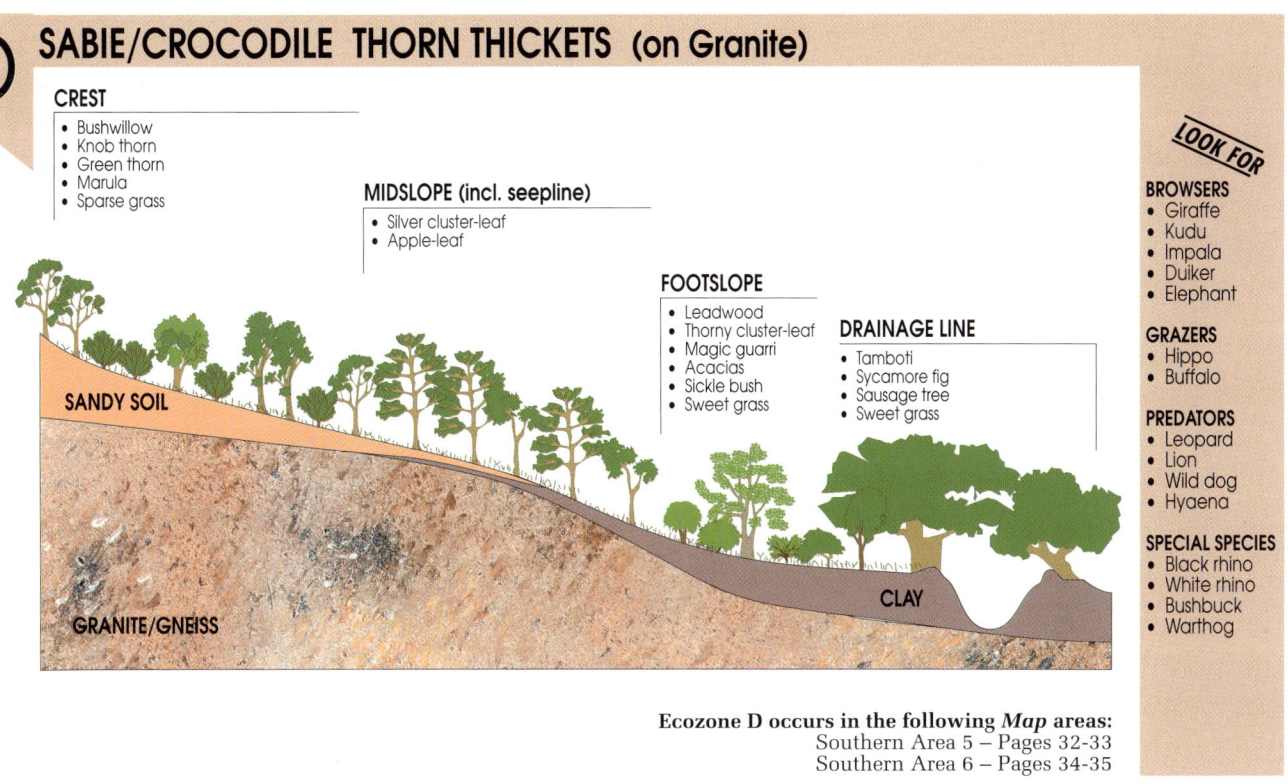

D SABIE/CROCODILE THORN THICKETS (on Granite)

CREST
- Bushwillow
- Knob thorn
- Green thorn
- Marula
- Sparse grass

MIDSLOPE (incl. seepline)
- Silver cluster-leaf
- Apple-leaf

FOOTSLOPE
- Leadwood
- Thorny cluster-leaf
- Magic guarri
- Acacias
- Sickle bush
- Sweet grass

DRAINAGE LINE
- Tamboti
- Sycamore fig
- Sausage tree
- Sweet grass

SANDY SOIL

GRANITE/GNEISS

CLAY

LOOK FOR

BROWSERS
- Giraffe
- Kudu
- Impala
- Duiker
- Elephant

GRAZERS
- Hippo
- Buffalo

PREDATORS
- Leopard
- Lion
- Wild dog
- Hyaena

SPECIAL SPECIES
- Black rhino
- White rhino
- Bushbuck
- Warthog

Ecozone D occurs in the following *Map* areas:
Southern Area 5 – Pages 32-33
Southern Area 6 – Pages 34-35

E THORN VELD (on Gabbro)

PLAINS
- Round-leafed teak
- Buffalo thorn
- Marula
- Large Knob thorn
- Sweet grass

DRAINAGE LINE
- Jackal berry
- Sycamore fig
- Magic guarri
- Sweet grass

GABBRO

DARK CLAY

LOOK FOR

BROWSERS
- Giraffe
- Kudu
- Impala
- Duiker

GRAZERS
- Zebra
- Wildebeest
- Buffalo

PREDATORS
- Cheetah
- Lion
- Hyaena
- Black-backed jackal

SPECIAL SPECIES
- Sable
- Warthog

Ecozone E occurs in the following *Map* areas:
Northern Area 2 – Pages 26-27
Central Area 3 – Pages 28-29
Central Area 4 – Pages 30-31
Southern Area 5 – Pages 32-33
Southern Area 6 – Pages 34-35

41

KNOB THORN/MARULA SAVANNAH (on Basalt)

LOOK FOR

BROWSERS
- Giraffe
- Kudu
- Steenbok

GRAZERS
- Wildebeest
- Zebra
- Buffalo
- Waterbuck

PREDATORS
- Cheetah
- Lion
- Hyaena
- Black-backed jackal

SPECIAL SPECIES
- Sable
- Warthog
- Ostrich

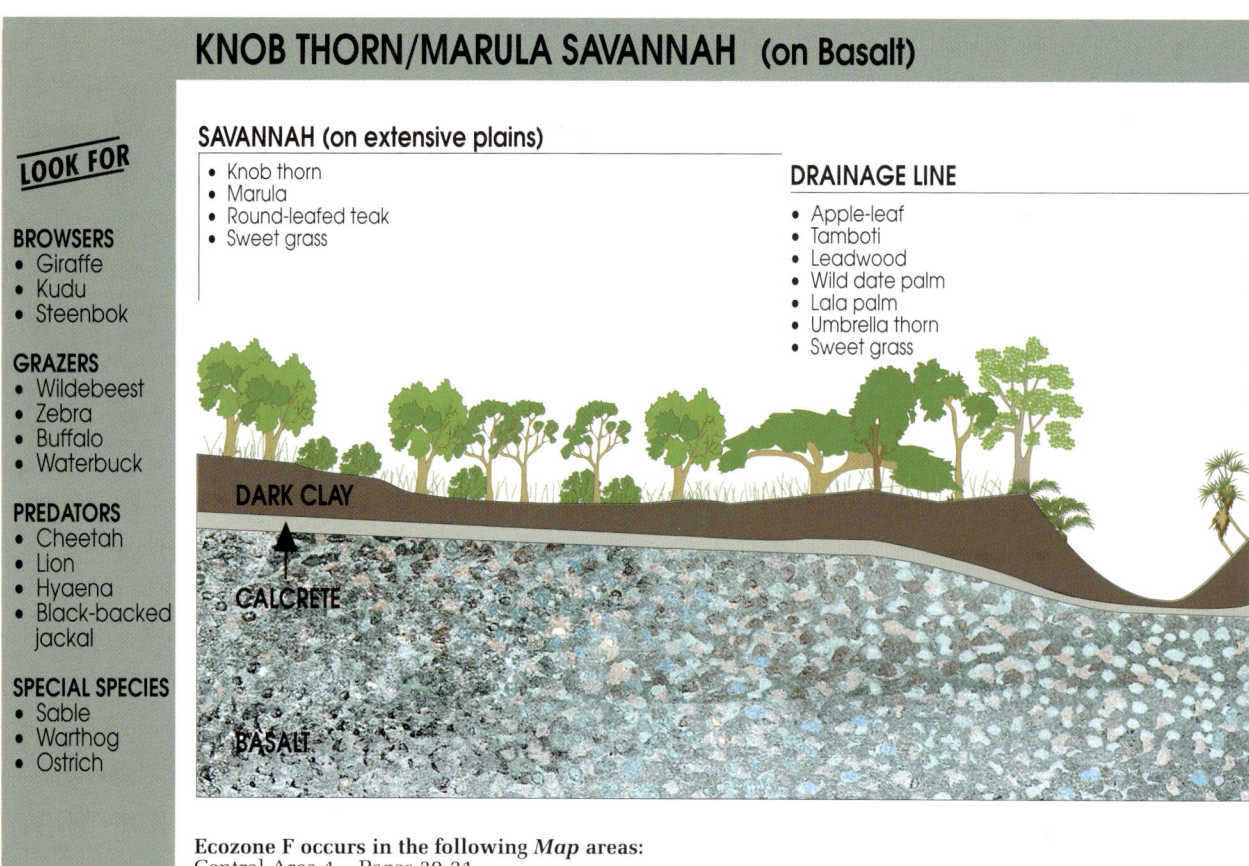

SAVANNAH (on extensive plains)
- Knob thorn
- Marula
- Round-leafed teak
- Sweet grass

DRAINAGE LINE
- Apple-leaf
- Tamboti
- Leadwood
- Wild date palm
- Lala palm
- Umbrella thorn
- Sweet grass

DARK CLAY

CALCRETE

BASALT

Ecozone F occurs in the following *Map* areas:
Central Area 4 – Pages 30-31
Southern Area 5 – Pages 32-33
Southern Area 6 – Pages 34-35

DELAGOA THORN THICKETS (on Ecca Shales)

LOOK FOR

BROWSERS
- Giraffe
- Kudu
- Impala
- Duiker
- Elephant

GRAZERS
- Wildebeest
- Zebra
- Waterbuck
- Buffalo

PREDATORS
- Cheetah
- Lion
- Leopard
- Hyaena

SPECIAL SPECIES
- White rhino

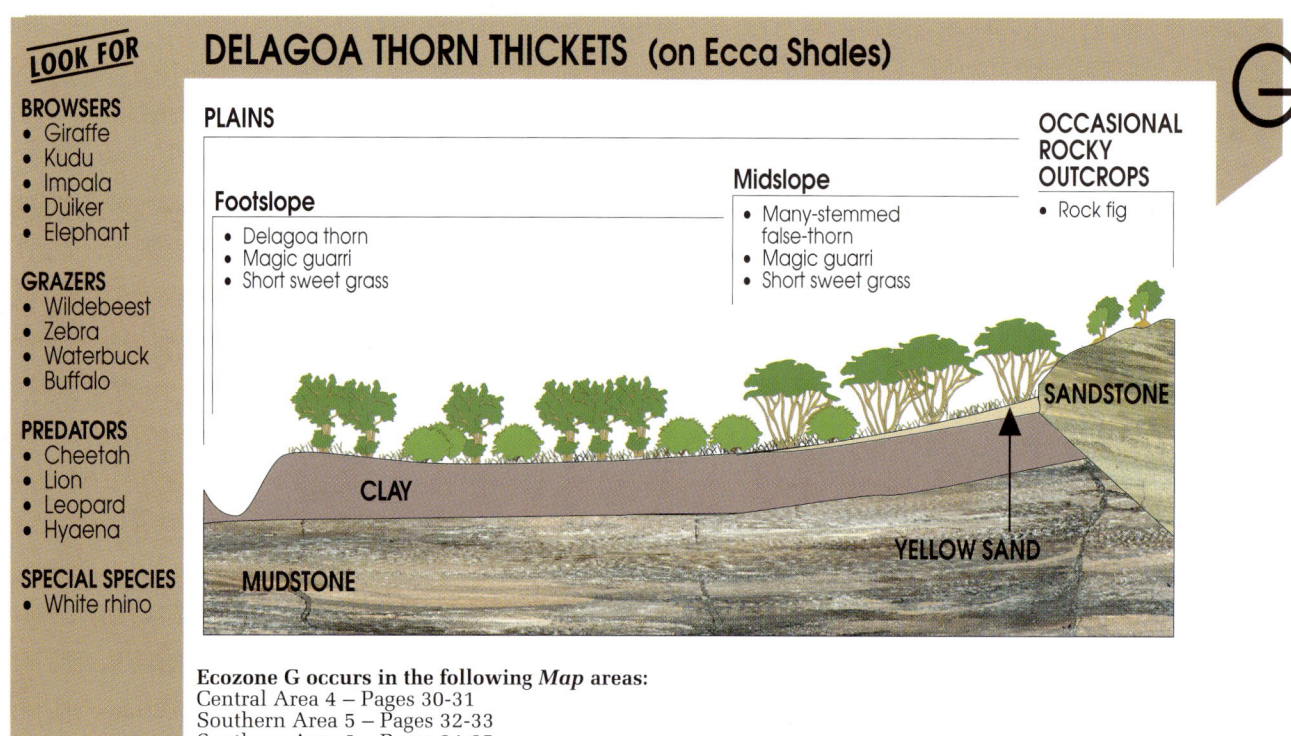

PLAINS

OCCASIONAL ROCKY OUTCROPS
- Rock fig

Footslope
- Delagoa thorn
- Magic guarri
- Short sweet grass

Midslope
- Many-stemmed false-thorn
- Magic guarri
- Short sweet grass

SANDSTONE

CLAY

YELLOW SAND

MUDSTONE

Ecozone G occurs in the following *Map* areas:
Central Area 4 – Pages 30-31
Southern Area 5 – Pages 32-33
Southern Area 6 – Pages 34-35

H RIVERINE COMMUNITIES

RIVER BANKS
- Sycamore fig
- Weeping boer-bean
- Matumi
- Sweet grass

RIVER BANKS
- Brack thorn
- Jackal berry
- Nyala tree (north)
- Buffalo thorn
- Wild date palm
- Reeds
- Sweet grass

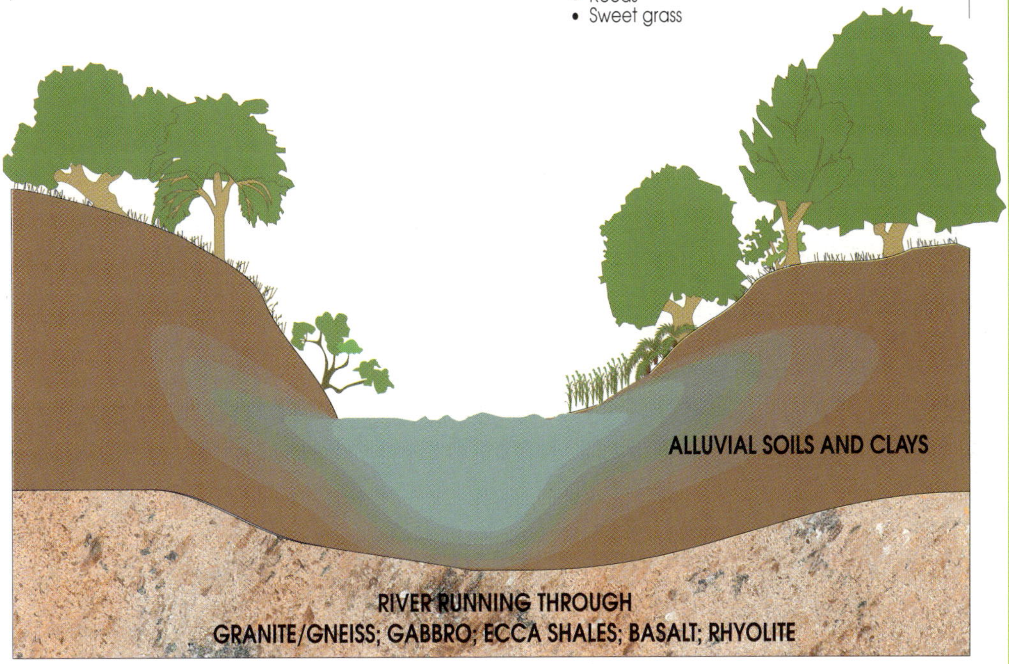

Riverine communities run alongside rivers and stretch across many other Ecozones.

Most animals cross this Ecozone at times, because of the water.

Animals named here are those that always prefer the riverine habitat for food and shelter.

LOOK FOR

BROWSERS
- Duiker

GRAZERS
- Hippo
- Waterbuck

PREDATORS
- Leopard

SPECIAL SPECIES
- Nyala (north)
- Bushbuck
- Clawless otter

ALLUVIAL SOILS
- Soils that are deposited by a river

ALLUVIAL SOILS AND CLAYS

RIVER RUNNING THROUGH
GRANITE/GNEISS; GABBRO; ECCA SHALES; BASALT; RHYOLITE

On the **Maps** Ecozone H is colour-coded green only and the letter reference has been omitted.

Ecozone H occurs in the following Map areas:
Northern Area 1 — Pages 24-25
Northern Area 2 — Pages 26-27
Central Area 3 — Pages 28-29
Central Area 4 — Pages 30-31
Southern Area 5 — Pages 32-33
Southern Area 6 — Pages 34-35

I LEBOMBO MOUNTAIN BUSHVELD (on Rhyolite)

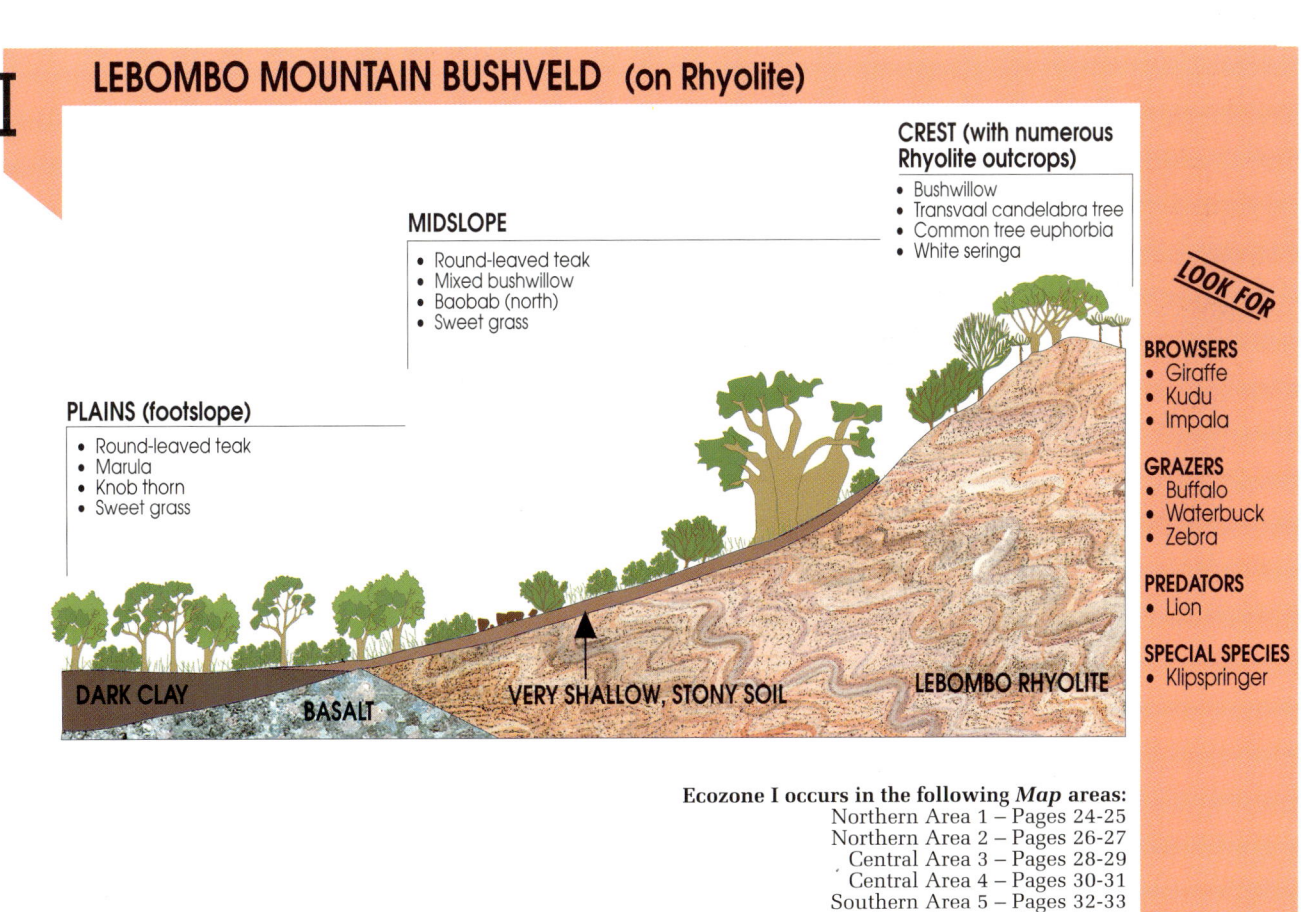

CREST (with numerous Rhyolite outcrops)
- Bushwillow
- Transvaal candelabra tree
- Common tree euphorbia
- White seringa

MIDSLOPE
- Round-leaved teak
- Mixed bushwillow
- Baobab (north)
- Sweet grass

PLAINS (footslope)
- Round-leaved teak
- Marula
- Knob thorn
- Sweet grass

LOOK FOR

BROWSERS
- Giraffe
- Kudu
- Impala

GRAZERS
- Buffalo
- Waterbuck
- Zebra

PREDATORS
- Lion

SPECIAL SPECIES
- Klipspringer

DARK CLAY   BASALT   VERY SHALLOW, STONY SOIL   LEBOMBO RHYOLITE

Ecozone I occurs in the following Map areas:
Northern Area 1 — Pages 24-25
Northern Area 2 — Pages 26-27
Central Area 3 — Pages 28-29
Central Area 4 — Pages 30-31
Southern Area 5 — Pages 32-33
Southern Area 6 — Pages 34-35

43

OLIFANTS RUGGED VELD (on Rhyolite/Basalt)

CREST
- White seringa
- Bushwillow
- Transvaal candelabra tree
- Sparse grass

MIDSLOPE
- Knob thorn
- Thorny cluster-leaf
- Bushwillow
- Raisin bush
- Mixed grass

DRAINAGE LINE
- Sycamore fig
- Leadwood
- Fever tree
- Sweet grass

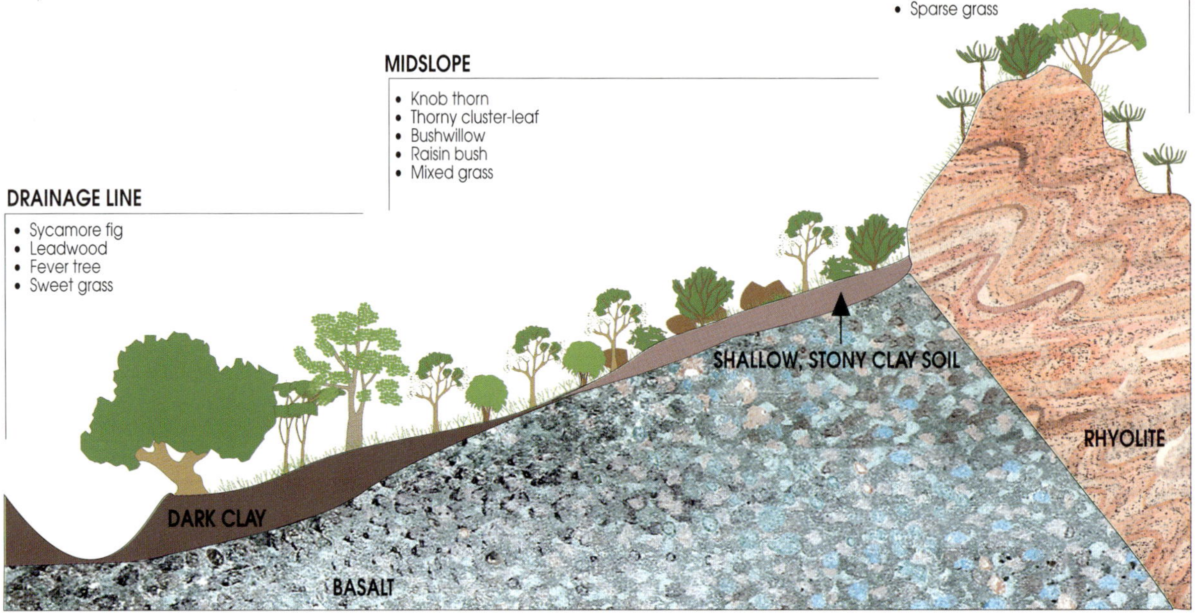

LOOK FOR

BROWSERS
- Impala
- Kudu
- Elephant
- Giraffe

GRAZERS
- Waterbuck
- Zebra

PREDATORS
- Lion
- Hyaena

SPECIAL SPECIES
- Klipspringer

SHALLOW, STONY CLAY SOIL

RHYOLITE

DARK CLAY

BASALT

Ecozone J occurs in the following *Map* areas:
Central Area 4 – Pages 30-31

STUNTED KNOB THORN SAVANNAH (on Basalt)

K

DRAINAGE LINE
- Jackal berry
- Sycamore fig
- Fever tree
- Sweet grass

FOOTSLOPE
- Umbrella thorn
- Magic guarri
- Leadwood
- Sweet grass

CREST (extensive plains)
- Stunted Knob thorn
- Mixed grass

LOOK FOR

BROWSERS
- Giraffe
- Kudu
- Impala

GRAZERS
- Zebra
- Wildebeest
- Buffalo

PREDATORS
- Cheetah
- Lion
- Hyaena

SPECIAL SPECIES
- Sable

DARK CLAY

CALCRETE

BASALT

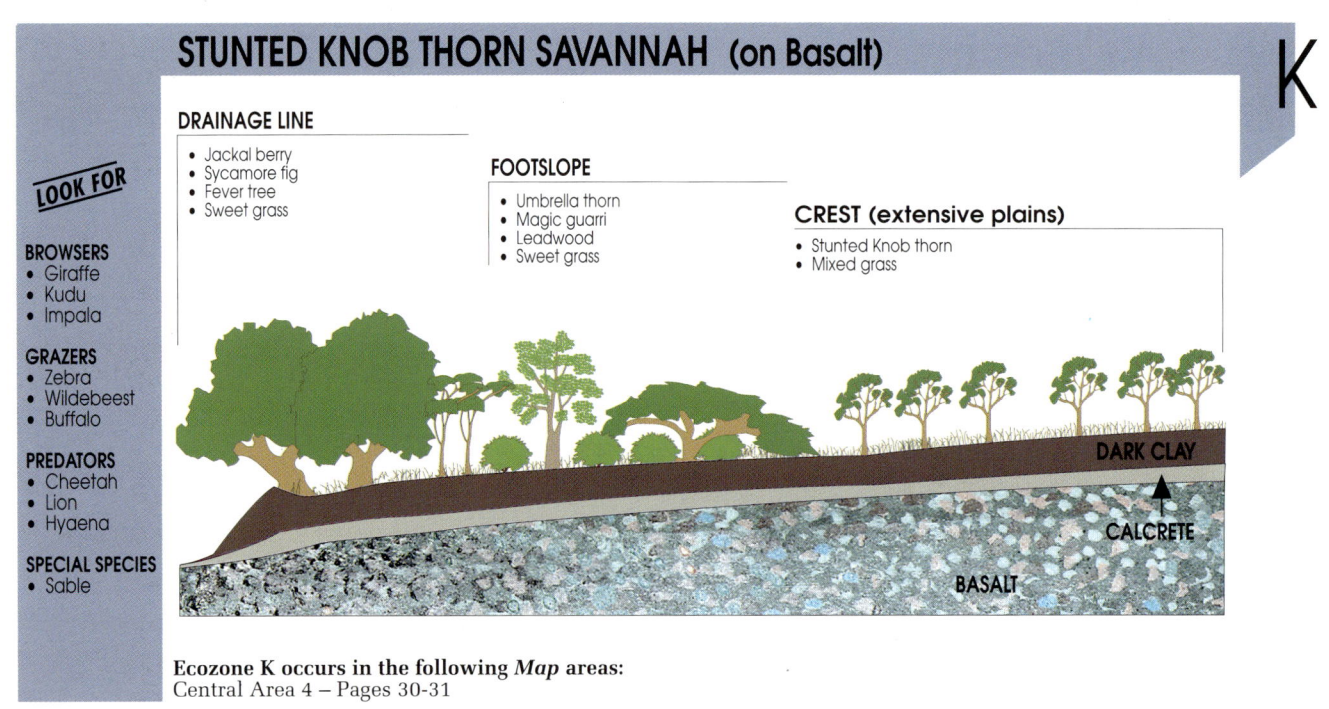

Ecozone K occurs in the following *Map* areas:
Central Area 4 – Pages 30-31

L MOPANE SHRUBVELD (on Basalt)

-------- South of Klopperfontein --------   -------- North of Klopperfontein --------

EXTENSIVE, FLAT PLAINS
- Apple-leaf
- Shrub Mopane
- Mixed grass

DRAINAGE LINE
- Large Knob thorn
- Tamboti
- Leadwood
- Apple-leaf
- Sweet grass

DRAINAGE LINE
- Tamboti
- Leadwood
- Apple-leaf
- Nyala tree
- Sweet grass

UNDULATING PLAINS
- Thorny cluster-leaf
- Baobab
- Shrub Mopane
- Mixed grass

SHALLOW CLAY

CALCRETE

SHALLOW CLAY

CALCRETE

BASALT

BASALT

LOOK FOR

BROWSERS
- Elephant, Steenbok

GRAZERS
- Buffalo, Wildebeest, Zebra

PREDATORS
- Cheetah, Lion, Black-backed jackal

SPECIAL SPECIES
- Eland, Tsessebe, Roan, Sable, Ostrich, Side-striped jackal

Ecozone L occurs in the following *Map* areas:
Northern Area 1 – Pages 24-25
Northern Area 2 – Pages 26-27
Central Area 3 – Pages 28-29
Central Area 4 – Pages 30-31

M ALLUVIAL PLAINS

Alluvial plains are created by the soils that are brought down by flooding rivers. They border all major rivers and water courses. The plains are best developed where the rivers cross the Basalts.

The availability of water influences the types and sizes of trees, as flood water spreads over these plains.
Good examples of this Ecozone can be seen at Shingwedzi and Pafuri.

TREES
- Sausage tree
- Weeping boer-bean
- Natal mahogany
- Brack thorn
- Transvaal mustard tree

GRASSES
- Sparse, short sweet grass

BROWSERS
- Impala
- Kudu
- Duiker

GRAZERS
- Buffalo
- Waterbuck

PREDATORS
- Leopard
- Lion

SPECIAL SPECIES
- Bushbuck
- Nyala
- Sharpe's grysbok (Shingwedzi)

Ecozone M occurs in the following *Map* areas:
Northern Area 1 – Pages 24-25
Northern Area 2 – Pages 26-27

N SANDVELD COMMUNITIES

These areas are generally sandy, and therefore well drained. Several natural springs occur.
The plant communities are very complex. No single tree dominates, but several species here are unique to the Park .

TREES
- White seringa
- Mixed bushwillow
- Silver cluster-leaf
- Baobab
- Pod mahogany
- Sickle bush
- Weeping wattle

GRASSES
- Sparse to moderate sweet grass

BROWSERS
- Kudu
- Impala
- Giraffe

GRAZERS
- Zebra
- Buffalo

PREDATORS
- Wild dog
- Lion
- Hyaena

SPECIAL SPECIES
- Nyala
- Sharpe's grysbok

Ecozone N occurs in the following *Map* areas:
Northern Area 1 – Pages 24-25
Northern Area 2 – Pages 26-27
Central Area 3 – Pages 28-29
Central Area 4 – Pages 30-31

TREE MOPANE SAVANNAH (on Ecca Shales)

O

LOOK FOR

BROWSERS
• Kudu
• Elephant
• Impala
• Duiker

GRAZERS
• Buffalo

PREDATORS
• Lion
• Hyaena
• Wild dog

SPECIAL SPECIES
• Sharpe's grysbok
• Nyala
• Sable (south)

DRAINAGE LINE
• Mopane
• Magic guarri
• Tamboti
• Sweet grass

PLAINS
• Mopane
• Tamboti
• Sweet grass

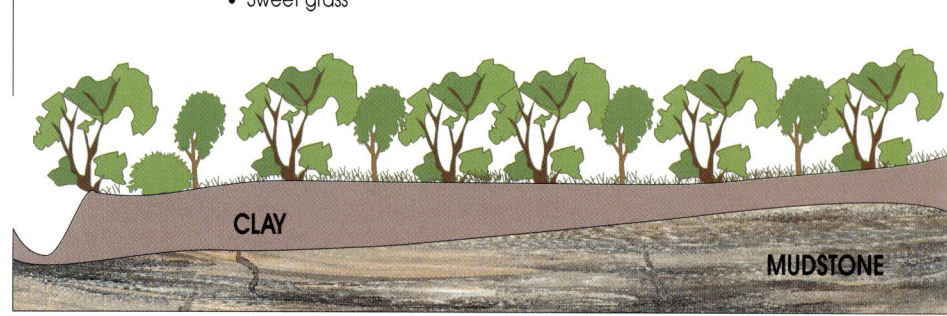

CLAY

MUDSTONE

Ecozone O occurs in the following *Map* areas:
Northern Area 1 – Pages 24-25

MOPANE/BUSHWILLOW WOODLANDS (on Granite)

P

LOOK FOR

BROWSERS
• Kudu
• Impala
• Giraffe
• Elephant

GRAZERS
• Wildebeest
• Zebra
• Buffalo

PREDATORS
• Lion
• Hyaena

SPECIAL SPECIES
• Sable
• Eland

CREST
• Mixed Bushwillow
• Mopane (only on termite mounds – clay)
• Mixed grass

MIDSLOPE (incl. seepline)
• Silver cluster-leaf
• Mixed Bushwillow
• Mixed grass

FOOTSLOPE
• Mopane
• Large Knob thorn
• Mixed Acacias
• Mixed grass

DRAINAGE LINE
• Apple-leaf
• Leadwood
• Sweet grass

SAND

GRANITE/GNEISS

CLAY

Ecozone P occurs in the following *Map* areas:
Northern Area 1 – Pages 24-25
Northern Area 2 – Pages 26-27
Central Area 3 – Pages 28-29
Central Area 4 – Pages 30-31

FIND IT

GEOLOGY

How the Lowveld was formed

The Kruger National Park has a fascinating variety of rocks, from some of the oldest known on earth to some of the youngest. And it is all there for you to see.

The earth's surface is changing constantly, but in most cases very slowly.

The rocks below the surface also undergo significant shifts and radical alterations over millions of years.

3 500 – 200 million years ago

The most ancient rocks are older than 3 500 million years. The most common of these are Granite/Gneiss with intrusions of Gabbro.

As a result of a wet, marshy period (about 300 – 200 million years ago), Ecca Shales were laid down on the Granite/Gneiss and Gabbro base.

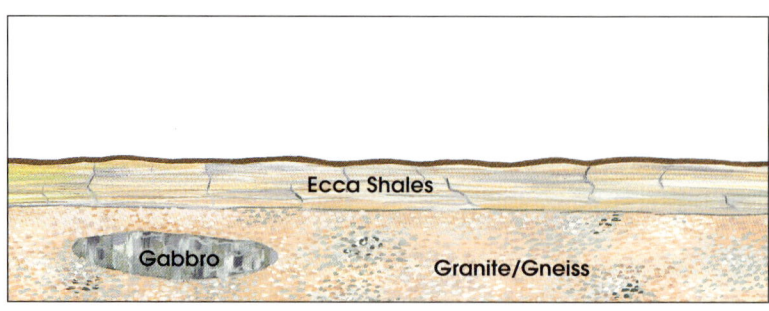

200 – 135 million years ago

The huge primitive Gondwanaland continent started breaking up about 200 million years ago. This break-up was associated with volcanic activity.

Molten rock burst through the crusts of the earth to form layers of Basalt.

Further volcanic activity led to Rhyolite being laid down on top of the Basalt (about 180 million years ago).

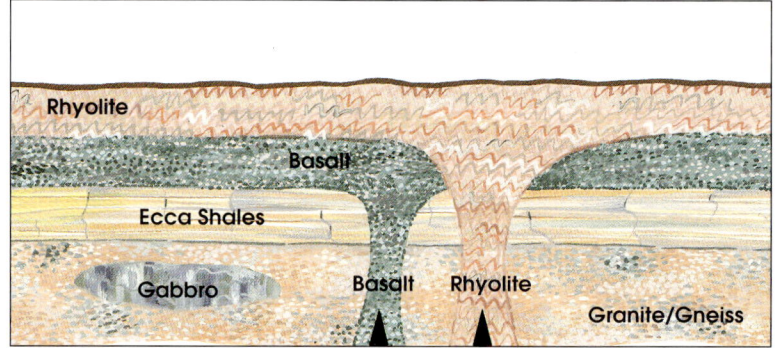

With the breaking up of Gondwanaland, the original flat beds of Granite/Gneiss, Ecca Shales, Basalt and Rhyolite split apart (about 135 million years ago). The eastern half of Southern Africa tilted towards the sea on the east.

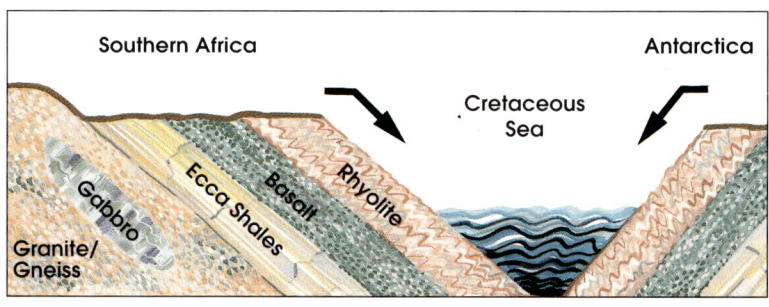

As the new continental edge and coastline of South East Africa developed, many of the present land-shape and ecosystems of the KNP had their beginning.

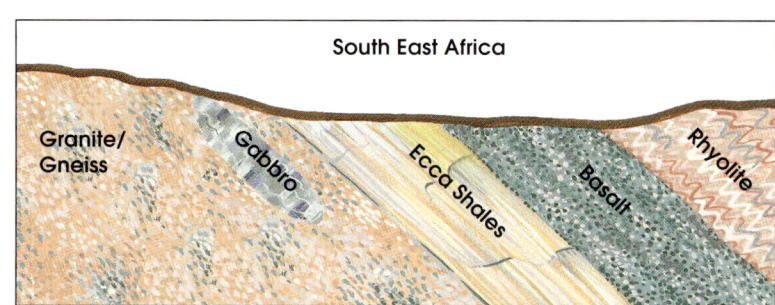

The Lowveld as it is today

The escarpment and Malelane Mountains (in the west) and the Lebombo Mountains (in the east) were the most resistant to the forces of erosion by wind, rain and rivers. They therefore maintained a higher altitude than the rest of the Lowveld.

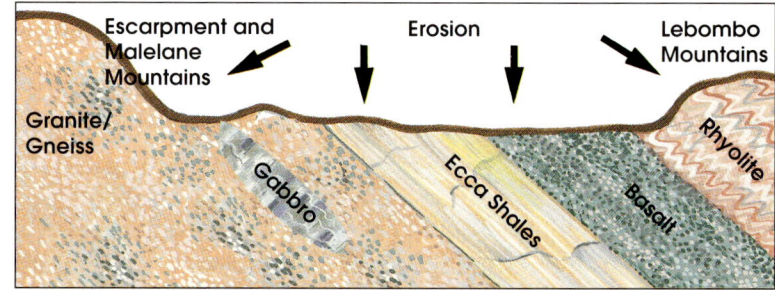

Geological sites

The following geological sites are easy to find. They are marked here and on the Kruger National Park *Maps* (pages 24-35) with ⚲. The shapes, colours and general structure of the rock formations are interesting to look at and could help you to identify the surrounding plants and animals.

1 Flat-lying, dark-grey flows of **Basalt**

2-3 Light-brown **Clarens Sandstone**, originally formed as massive sand dunes

4-6 Resistant exposures of old, light-brown and red **Soutpansberg Quartzites**

7 Potholed, red **Clarens Sandstone** (Red Rocks)

8 Prominent hills and koppies of columnar, jointed, grey **Gabbro** (Tshanga look-out point)

9 Vertical, grey **Dolerite** dykes

10 Prominent, light-coloured **Granophyre** (ridges at Shibavantsengele)

11 Dark-grey **Nephelinite** rocks, representing ancient volcanic plugs

12 Off-white, coarse **Clarens Sandstone**

13-14 Coarse-grained, orange-coloured **Syenite** plugs (Shikumbu and Masorini)

15 Prominent exposure of blocky, grey **Gabbro**

16 Grey and pink **Granite/Gneiss** cut by light-coloured pegmatite veins

17 Dark-green and black **Greenstone** outcrops

18 Dark-grey **Basalt** flows in river banks and road cuttings (Letaba River and Road S47)

19 Prominent, vertical, light-coloured **Rhyolite** dyke (Shamiriri, extending south to Olifants River)

20 Vertical, grey **Dolerite** dyke

21 Olifants rest camp situated on prominent **Rhyolite** dome

22 Off-white, coarse **Clarens Sandstone** (at picnic-site)

23 Outcrops of reddish **Rhyolite** cut by orange **Granophyre** dykes

24 Off-white, coarse **Clarens Sandstone**

25-27 Prominent, orange-coloured **Granophyre** ridges (N'Wamuriwa, Nkumbe, Muntshe)

28 Bedded, grey **Ecca Shales** and **Mudstone** in river-bank

29 Easterly-dipping, light-coloured **Clarens Sandstone** dune beds (Lubyelubye bridge)

30 Grey **Basalt** flows, cut by **Dolerite** dykes

31-34 Prominent, ancient **Granite/Gneiss** koppies (Grano Kop)

35 Prominent outcrop of blocky, grey **Gabbro**

36 Prominent, ancient **Granite/Gneiss** koppies (Shabeni Kop)

37 Blocky, grey **Gabbro** (Ship Mountain)

38 Ridges and koppies of pink and grey-banded **Granite/Gneiss**

39 Outcrop of dark-coloured **Greenstone**

40 Prominent hillside exposure of dark and light-banded **Granite/Gneiss** (Tlhalabye)

41 Outcrop of dark-coloured **Greenstone**

42 Coarse, light-brown **Clarens Sandstone** outcrops

Remember to refer to the Ecozone pages (39-46) to see which Ecozones have the same underlying geology.

Legend

- Gabbro
- Granite/Gneiss
- Ecca Shales
- Basalt
- Rhyolite
- Other geological formations

Map labels

PAFURI, PUNDA MARIA, SHINGWEDZI, MOPANI, LETABA, PHALABORWA, OLIFANTS, SATARA, ORPEN, PAUL KRUGER, SKUKUZA, NUMBI, PRETORIUSKOP, BERG-EN-DAL, LOWER SABIE, CROCODILE BRIDGE, MALELANE

49

Travel through time

In the Kruger National Park you can see some fascinating geology, and you can also travel on an adventure through time! In the west, some of the ancient Granite is 3 500 million years old. In the east, the relatively young Basalt and Rhyolite were formed less than 200 million years ago.

Drive along the H7 between Orpen and Satara and along the H6 (or S100) between Satara and N'wanetsi.

As you travel, notice the changes in:

❏ geology ❏ shape of the land ❏ plants ❏ animal distribution

3 500 – 200 million years

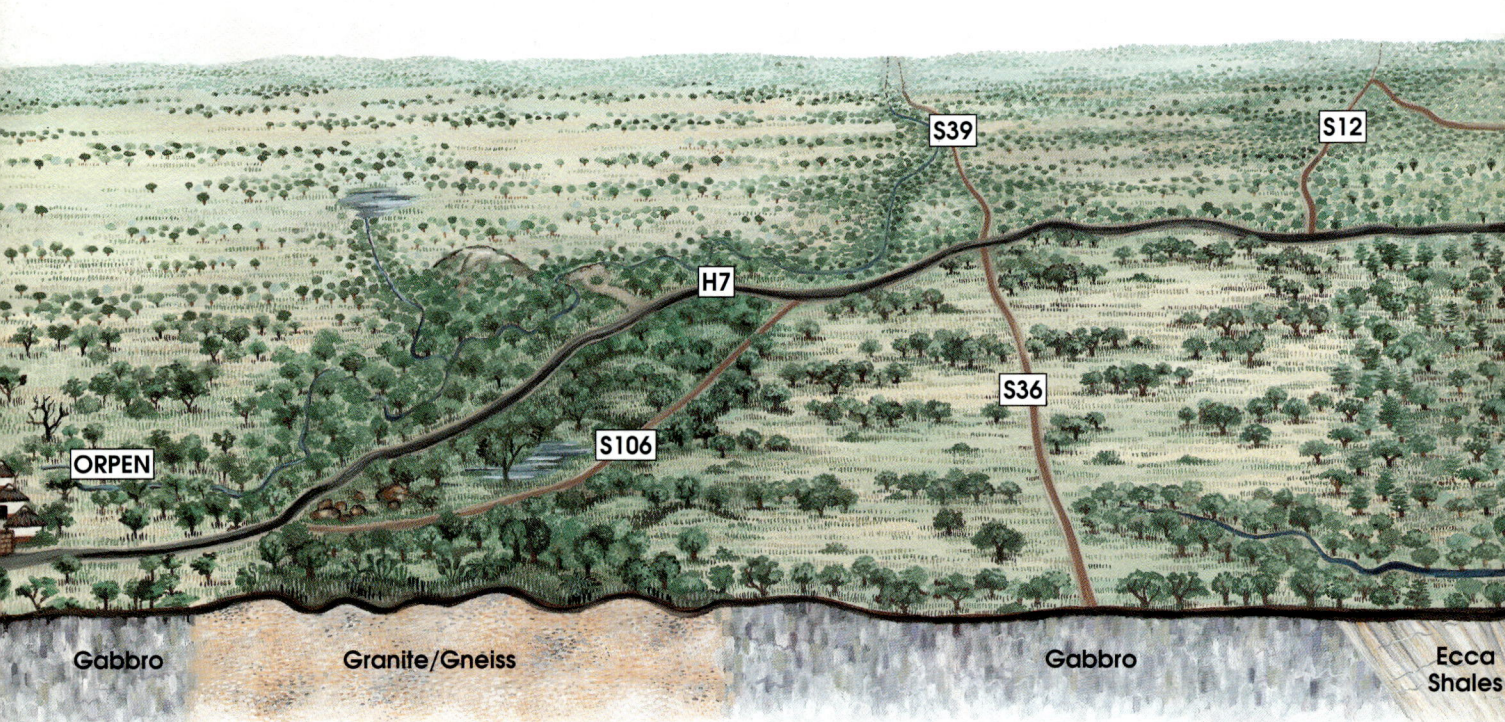

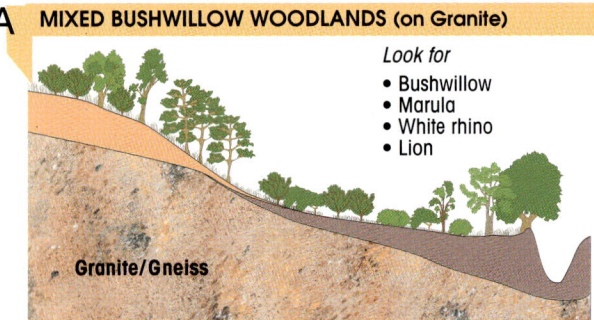

Granite/Gneiss

The underlying Granite/Gneiss gives rise to gently rolling hills. These are formed by rocks that are more resistant to erosion, and therefore stand out above the surrounding areas.

Many drainage lines (rivers and spruits) can be seen in granitic areas which are caused by uneven weathering.

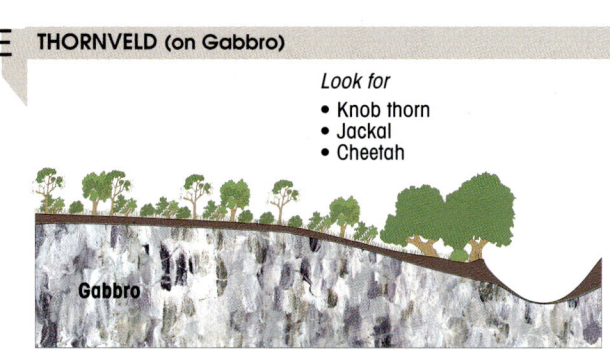

Gabbro

These ancient rocks weather to form very fertile soil.

The Gabbro near Orpen underlies open, flat plains of sweet grass. Large numbers of herbivores can often be seen.

Ecca Shales

This area is very flat and wa[ter] does not penetra[te] the soils easily.

Remember! Wherever you are in the KNP, you can use your *Maps*, Ecozone diagrams and *Find It* to see more!

50

Altitude and rainfall

Each Ecozone is an area with its own geology, rainfall, altitude and land-shape.

Look at the rainfall map on the right to see how this relates to some of the Ecozones of the Kruger National Park.

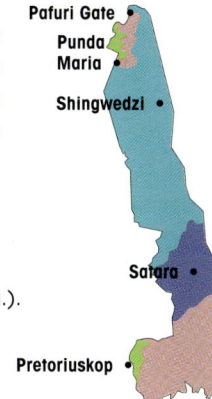

🟦	400-500 mm
🟪	500-600 mm
🟫	600-700 mm
🟩	700-800 mm

Pafuri Gate
Punda Maria
Shingwedzi
Satara
Pretoriuskop

Altitude

The KNP is generally flat to undulating, with the central region averaging 260 m above sea level.

The only higher areas are the Lebombo Mountains in the east, the hills near Punda Maria in the north and the Malelane Mountains in the south. Khandzalive (near Malelane) is the highest point at 839 m above sea level.

Rainfall

The KNP is a summer rainfall area (September to March), with an overall average of 500 mm per annum. The rain is often in the form of thunder-storms.

Rainfall generally decreases from the south to the north, and from the west to the east with Pafuri having the lowest average (440 mm p.a.).

Pretoriuskop (740 mm p.a.) and Punda Maria (600 mm p.a.) are the highest rainfall areas.

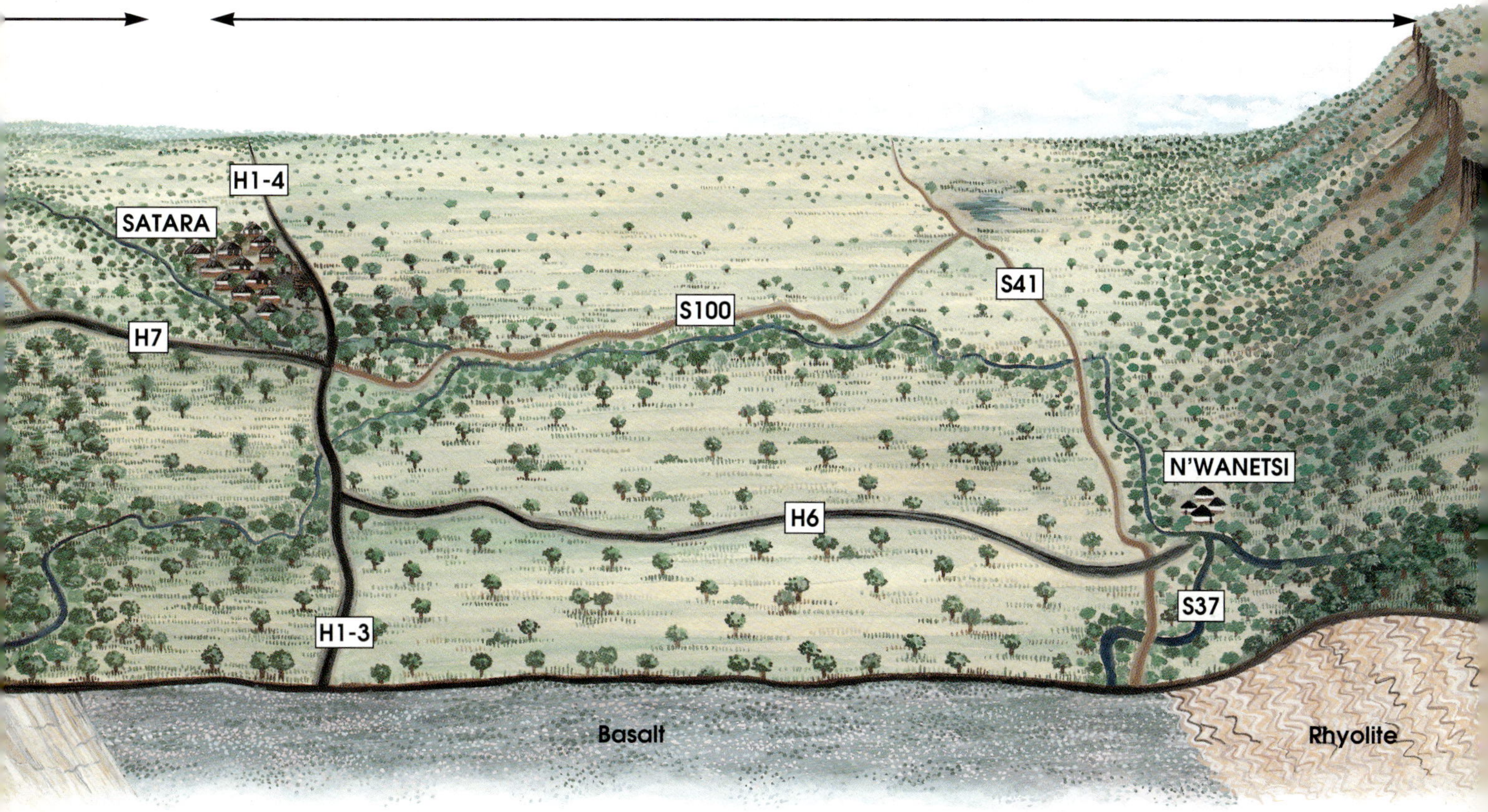

200 – 135 million years

Basalt

Rhyolite

THICKETS (on Ecca Shales)

Look for
- goa thorn
- e rhino

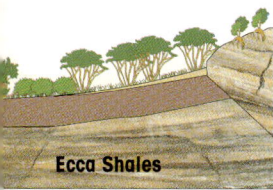

Ecca Shales

re many pans tend to form.
ozone has vegetation that
nowhere else in the KNP.
ss is generally short
eet.

KNOB THORN/MARULA SAVANNAH (on Basalt)

Look for
- Knob thorn
- Hyaena
- Waterbuck

Basalt

Basalt

Underlying Basalt gives rise to very flat plains with few drainage lines.

Vegetation is less variable than in the Granites, but the grass is sweet as a result of the high nutrient value of the clay soil.

LEBOMBO MOUNTAIN BUSHVELD (on Rhyolite)

Look for
- Euphorbia
- Leopard
- Klipspringer

Rhyolite

Rhyolite

Rhyolite is more resistant to weathering than Basalt and forms the Lebombo Mountain range.

Throughout the KNP you can see examples of the fascinating geological formations. These are listed in detail on page 49.

PLANTS

There are thousands of varieties of plants in the Kruger National Park. They are fascinating in their own right – but are also of great interest because of the never-ending cycle of interaction between plant and animal worlds.

There are two types of plants which offer food to animals:

- ❏ **Grasses**
- ❏ **Non-grasses –** trees, shrubs, climbers and forbs

All plants (whether grasses or others) vary in their attraction as food depending on:
- ❏ how tasty they are
- ❏ how high the actual food value is

You will find different animals in different areas of the Kruger, according to the food they eat.

Animals that eat plants are called herbivores. Herbivores can generally be divided into two groups:

- ❏ **Grazers** that mostly eat grasses
- ❏ **Browsers** that mostly eat non-grasses

A few animals, like impala and elephant, graze **and** browse. Their choice will depend on which plants offer the best quality food in an area.

Different grazers eat different types of grass in the varying seasons. However, they do have a preference about the height of the grass they graze. Roan and sable feed off taller grasses. Wildebeest prefer very short grasses, and therefore often follow zebra that graze medium-height grasses.

Grass savannah provides food for a large number of animals. Therefore grazers are often herd animals.

Bees and many insects pollinate specific plants. Without this interaction these plants would not reproduce and the food source would rapidly die out.

52

Different browsers eat at different heights and from different types of plants. Browsers generally obtain food from softer leaves, bark, flowers and pods.

Watch an elephant carefully as he browses on a shrub or tree. You will see him break off a small branch, roll it in his mouth and eat the bark off the stem.

Watch a giraffe use her long, careful tongue to select the tender leaves from amongst the thorns of an Acacia.

Small antelope, like steenbok and duiker, are generally browsers. They tend to eat forbs which are lower on the ground.

Forbs are plants that normally sprout profusely soon after rain and die back at the end of summer (annuals). They rarely grow as tall as the shrubs and trees that live for many years (perennials).

Wooded, bushy areas cannot feed as many animals as the same size grassland. Browsers therefore tend to be solitary or in small groups.

Termites carry dry grasses and leaves below the surface of the ground into the termitaria (anthills/ termite mounds). This fertilises and aerates the soil.

The recycling of plant material is essential to ensure that the food taken out of the soil by vegetation is returned for future growth.

The following pages describe the grasses and trees that visitors are most likely to see at the Kruger National Park.

53

Grasses and reeds

The kind of grazer you are likely to see partly depends on the state and the species of grass in that area.

Animals choose to graze a specific grass depending on its palatability (taste).

Species of grass have different levels of taste and food value, depending on:

- ❏ type of grass
- ❏ soil where it grows
- ❏ amount of rainfall in the area
- ❏ amount of rainfall that season
- ❏ age of the specific plant
  (some grasses are only palatable and nutritious while they are young)

You should see more grazers where grass is palatable and nutritious.

"Mixed grass" in the Ecozones (pages 39-46) refers to an area where both "sweet" and "sour" grass grows.

Areas where grass tends to be palatable and nutritious throughout the year are called "sweet" grassveld areas.

Where grass grows fast and tall, rainfall is normally high. This grass usually become fibrous and unpalatable when it matures. These areas are known as "Sourveld" areas, such as the Ecozone B on the **Maps** (Pretoriuskop Sourveld).

 **Further reading:**
Guide to Grasses of South Africa – Frits van Oudtshoorn

Grasses – Group A

These grasses are generally palatable and nutritious – "sweet" grasses – eaten by most grazers. These species decrease with over-utilization.

Finger grass
Digitaria eriantha
Up to 1,4 m; perennial
Habitat: Open areas on most soils, especially sandy areas
Seed: Jan – Apr
Utilization: Extensive

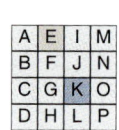

Blue buffalo grass
Cenchrus ciliaris
Up to 1 m; perennial
Habitat: Occurs on most soils; on termitaria
Seed: Aug – Apr
Utilization: Very palatable when young

Guinea grass
Panicum maximum
Up to 2,5 m; perennial
Habitat: All soils; damp places with fertile soil; shade of trees; along rivers
Seed: Nov – Jul
Utilization: Extensive, particularly white rhino

Vlei bristle grass
Setaria incrassata
Up to 2 m; perennial
Habitat: Basalt; Gabbro; heavy, clay soils; vleis & marshes
Seed: Oct – May
Utilization: Most grazers

Rooigras (Red grass)
Themeda triandra
0,3-1,5 m; perennial
Habitat: Basalt; Gabbro; Dolerite; undisturbed grassland areas
Seed: Oct – Jul
Utilization: Tall-grass grazers, like buffalo

Reeds – Group B

Reeds provide dry season grazing.

Reeds
Phragmites australis
Up to 4 m; perennial
Habitat: Near water; often form dense stands
Seed: Dec – Jun
Utilization: Buffalo, hippo & elephant, for dry season grazing

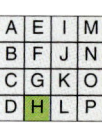

Grass is usually easy to identify by its seed-head (inflorescence). Most seed-heads develop during the summer months (September to April).

Grasses – Group C

These grasses are generally not palatable or nutritious
and are only eaten when young and tender.
These species increase with over-utilization.

A	E	I	M
B	F	J	N
C	G	K	O
D	H	L	P

Stinking grass
Bothriochloa radicans
Up to 0,7 m
Habitat: Drier Basalt areas;
heavy, clay soil; around termite
mounds; stony slopes
Seed: Oct – Apr
Utilization: Only when young

A	E	I	M
B	F	J	N
C	G	K	O
D	H	L	P

Grasses – Group D

These grasses are nutritious but only palatable
when young – "sour" grasses.
These species increase with under-utilization.

Spear grass
Heteropogon contortus
Up to 0,7 m; perennial; fast-growing grass
Habitat: Well-drained stony soils; open areas;
twisted seed-heads are often seen along roadsides
Seed: Oct – Jun
Utilization: Roan & waterbuck

Fine thatching grass
Hyparrhenia filipendula
Up to 1,5 m; perennial
Habitat: All soils; high rainfall;
near vleis & rivers
Seed: Nov – Apr
Utilization: Tall-grass feeders

A	E	I	M
B	F	J	N
C	G	K	O
D	H	L	P

Nine-awned grass
Enneapogon cenchroides
Up to 1 m; hardy grass that
withstands drought
Habitat: Sandy, soils; disturbed areas
Seed: Dec – May
Utilization: Fairly well when young

A	E	I	M
B	F	J	N
C	G	K	O
D	H	L	P

Cat's tail
Perotis patens
Up to 0,6 m
Habitat: Poor, sandy soils;
dry, bare patches;
disturbed areas
Seed: Nov – Apr

A	E	I	M
B	F	J	N
C	G	K	O
D	H	L	P

Yellow thatching grass
Hyperthelia dissoluta
Up to 3 m; very woody & tall; perennial
Habitat: Granitic, sandy soils; open areas;
higher rainfall; disturbed soils
Seed: Jan – Jun
Utilization: Tall-grass feeders

A	E	I	M
B	F	J	N
C	G	K	O
D	H	L	P

Broad-leaved
curly leaf
Eragrostis rigidior
Up to 1 m; perennial
Habitat: Sandy, loam soils;
open areas; disturbed soils
Seed: Oct – May

A	E	I	M
B	F	J	N
C	G	K	O
D	H	L	P

Creeping
bristle grass
Setaria sphacelata
Up to 0,5 m
Habitat: Granitic,
well-drained soils;
important in soil
conservation as it forms
runners which bind the soil
Seed: Sep – Mar

A	E	I	M
B	F	J	N
C	G	K	O
D	H	L	P

Utilization by animals refers to grazing.

Trees

This list covers some of the more important, common trees and shrubs in the Kruger National Park, as well as those which are easy for you to find.
It is not, however, a complete tree list by which you can identify every tree in the KNP.

Use these pages to identify common trees and shrubs easily.

- ❏ From your **Map** work out in which Ecozone you are.
- ❏ Read the diagram for your specific Ecozone to understand which trees can be found in the different habitats (e.g. on hill crests, valley bottoms etc.)

- ❏ Look up these trees in the **Find It.** The pictures and the comments will help you to form a mental picture of each tree.
- ❏ *Now try to find that specific tree, in that specific habitat... in the KNP!*

All trees listed below have a national tree number. These are the same as the numbers on some trees in the KNP. All deciduous trees are illustrated with summer foliage on the left side & bare winter branches on the right.

Further reading:
Field Guide to the Trees of the Kruger National Park – Piet van Wyk

Tree groups that are easy to recognise

Thorn trees (Acacias)

There are many different Acacias; some are easy to recognise. All Acacias have compound leaves, which are favoured by browsers & heavily thorned for protection against browsing. Tree shape, pod & thorn shape can help you to identify them.

This illustration represents the two Acacias described below.

168.1
Horned thorn
Acacia grandicornuta

9 m; deciduous
Thorns: Long (8 cm), straight, white (hard, sharp); in pairs
Flowers: Oct – Feb
Fruit: Mar – Sep
Utilization: Browsed; pods utilized by baboons & monkeys

A	E	I	M
B	F	J	N
C	G	K	O
D	H	L	P

179
Scented thorn
Acacia nilotica, subsp. *kraussiana*

Up to 7 m; deciduous
Trunk: Short, bare, crooked; divides low
Crown: Spreading round; branches hang downwards
Thorns: Long, slender, straight, white; in pairs
Flowers: Oct – Feb; round, bright-yellow, fragrant groups
Fruit: Mar – Sep; green-black; sticky; sweet-smelling, segmented
Utilization: Important browsing for smaller antelope

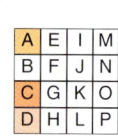

A	E	I	M
B	F	J	N
C	G	K	O
D	H	L	P

A	E	I	M
B	F	J	N
C	G	K	O
D	H	L	P

189
Fever tree
Acacia xanthophloea

Up to 15 m; deciduous
Trunk: Slender, bare, fairly high-branching
Bark: Unique, yellowy-green
Thorns: Long, white, slender; in pairs
Flowers: Aug – Sep; bright-yellow, dense, small balls
Fruit: Late summer; highly utilized
Utilization: Leaves, branches & gum extensively; often damaged by elephants

163
Delagoa thorn
Acacia welwitschii, subsp. *delagoensis*

Up to 15 m; deciduous
Trunk: Usually straight, high-branching but with many lateral twigs making low-down, untidy bush
Crown: Spreading; fairly dense, untidy appearance
Thorns: Paired, hooked, small, grey-black
Flowers: Nov – Jan; white, spikes in clusters
Fruit: May – Jul
Utilization: Important food plant for many browsers

A	E	I	M
B	F	J	N
C	G	K	O
D	H	L	P

183.1
Brack thorn
Acacia robusta, subsp. *clavigera*

Up to 20 m; deciduous
Trunk: Single; high-branching; branches stretch upwards
Bark: Dark-grey to black; rough, fissured
Crown: Very dense, very dark-green; conspicuous along major rivers for dark, tidy, upward-reaching appearance
Thorns: Long, straight, white; in pairs
Flowers: Late winter – early spring; small, light yellow-white, sweet-scented
Fruit: Late summer; almost sickle-shaped; burst open while on the tree; seeds fall much later
Utilization: Sometimes browsed by elephants & kudu

A	E	I	M
B	F	J	N
C	G	K	O
D	H	L	P

DIPS KUMLEBEN

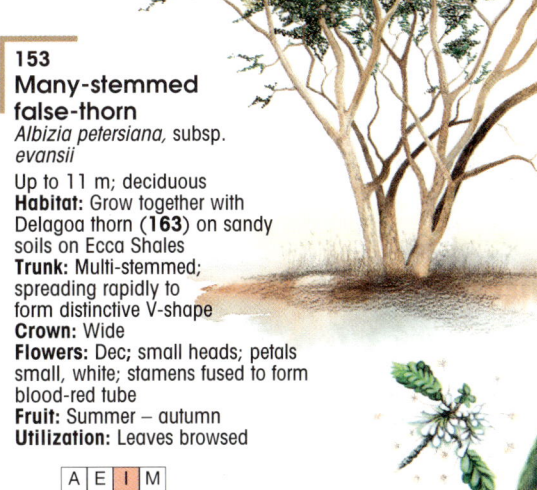

A	E	I	M
B	F	J	N
C	G	K	O
D	H	L	P

188
Umbrella thorn
Acacia tortilis, subsp. *heteracantha*

Up to 11 m; deciduous
Trunk: Short, branches out laterally to form umbrella shape
Thorns: Two kinds on each tree: small, brown, hooked; long, straight, white
Flowers: Nov – Dec; many white, round heads
Fruit: May – Jun
Utilization: Heavily browsed by all browsers
• **Very easy
to find**

A	E	I	M
B	F	J	N
C	G	K	O
D	H	L	P

178
Knob thorn
Acacia nigrescens

Up to 16 m; deciduous
Bark: Dark, grooved, rough
Leaves: Lacy, small, pale-green
Thorns: Knobs mainly grow on lower & younger branches, each tipped with a small, black, hooked thorn; initially thorns occur in pairs on branchlets
Flowers: Jun – Sep; many, small, white spikes
Fruit: Oct – Jan
Utilization: Heavily browsed, particularly by giraffe

False-thorn trees (Albizias)

Leaves are compound and often confused with Acacias; thornless.

154
Broad-pod false-thorn
Albizia forbesii

Up to 10 m; deciduous
Habitat: Usually along rivers
Trunk: Single, straight, mostly bare
Flowers: Oct – Nov; fairly large, fragile, puff-like, white; long stamens
Fruit: Late summer; dark-brown, twisted, ridged
Utilization: Browsed

A	E	I	M
B	F	J	N
C	G	K	O
D	H	L	P

A	E	I	M
B	F	J	N
C	G	K	O
D	H	L	P

153
Many-stemmed false-thorn
Albizia petersiana, subsp. *evansii*

Up to 11 m; deciduous
Habitat: Grow together with Delagoa thorn (**163**) on sandy soils on Ecca Shales
Trunk: Multi-stemmed; spreading rapidly to form distinctive V-shape
Crown: Wide
Flowers: Dec; small heads; petals small, white; stamens fused to form blood-red tube
Fruit: Summer – autumn
Utilization: Leaves browsed

Euphorbias

The Euphorbias have characteristic succulent-like thick, green branches, like chubby fingers.

346
Transvaal candelabra tree
Euphorbia cooperi

Up to 7 m
Trunk: Long, single, bare; branches arise from the trunk at a common point; lower branches die off annually, leaving holes in stem; latex extremely poisonous
Flowers: May – Aug; yellow-green
Fruit: Aug – Oct
Utilization: Not browsed; fruit eaten by seed-eating birds
• **Very easy to find**

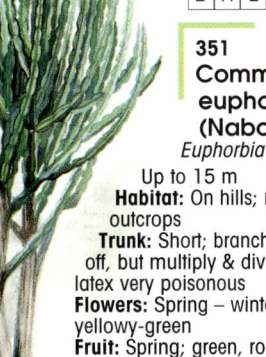

A	E	I	M
B	F	J	N
C	G	K	O
D	H	L	P

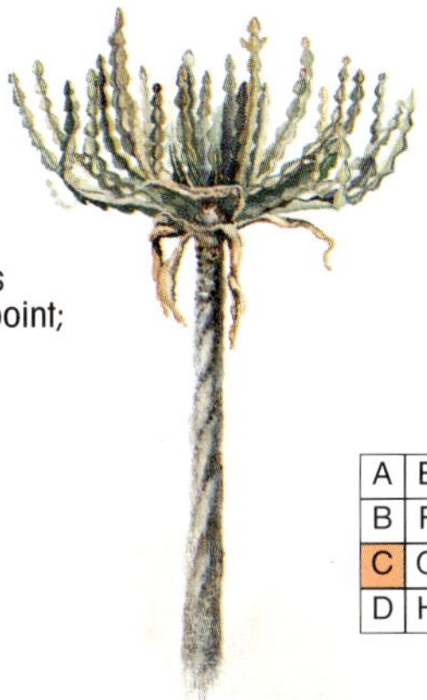

A	E	I	M
B	F	J	N
C	G	K	O
D	H	L	P

351
Common tree euphorbia (Naboom)
Euphorbia ingens

Up to 15 m
Habitat: On hills; rocky outcrops
Trunk: Short; branches do not die off, but multiply & divide; leafless; latex very poisonous
Flowers: Spring – winter; small yellowy-green
Fruit: Spring; green, roughly round
Utilization: Not browsed; fruit eaten by seed-eating birds
• **Very easy to find**

NOTE:
Many of these trees occur in a number of different Ecozones and in different habitats that are not mentioned here.

There they may grow differently and may be difficult to recognise from these descriptions.

This list is designed to introduce you to easily recognisable trees in their common habitats.

"Utilization" refers to the extent leaves and bark are eaten by browsers.

Bushwillows (Combretums)

Four common species of Combretum occur, three of which are similar.

Common features of Bushwillows

- ❏ Either low-branching with shortish, crooked stem; or no main trunk with multi-stem, having smaller branchlets growing up from the base
- ❏ Dense stands can cover large areas
- ❏ Usually deciduous
- ❏ Fruits four-winged
- ❏ No thorns

A	E	I	M
B	F	J	N
C	G	K	O
D	H	L	P

546
Large-fruited bushwillow
Combretum zeyheri
Up to 12 m; deciduous
Habitat: Granite & Rhyolite
Leaves: 8,5 x 4 cm
Fruit: Up to 6 cm diameter

Main differences between Bushwillows

- ❏ Size
- ❏ Habitat
- ❏ Size of leaves
- ❏ Size of fruits

A	E	I	M
B	F	J	N
C	G	K	O
D	H	L	P

538
Russet bushwillow
Combretum hereroense
Up to 8 m; deciduous
Habitat: Along rivers & streams; low-lying, rocky areas
Leaves: 3 x 2 cm
Flowers: Aug – Oct
Fruit: Midsummer; 2,3 x 2 cm; russet-brown colour

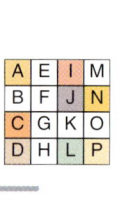

A	E	I	M
B	F	J	N
C	G	K	O
D	H	L	P

532
Red bushwillow
Combretum apiculatum,
subsp. *apiculatum*
Up to 9 m; deciduous
Habitat: Granitic & rhyolitic soils; rocky areas
Leaves: 6,5 x 3,5 cm
Flowers: Aug – Nov
Fruit: Summer – autumn; 2,5 x 2 cm

The Bushwillow illustrated here represents the three Bushwillows described above (532, 546, 538)

A	E	I	M
B	F	J	N
C	G	K	O
D	H	L	P

539
Leadwood
Combretum imberbe
Up to 20 m; deciduous
Habitat: Found everywhere in association with Knob thorn **(178)** and Marula **(360)**
Trunk: Single, thick, bare; extremely hard wood
Bark: Pale-grey, small, irregular, brick pattern
Crown: Old dead branchlets & branches do not break off easily; rather sparse foliage & small leaf for tree of this size
Flowers: Nov – Dec; small, yellow-green
Fruit: Autumn; small, brown-winged seeds
Utilization: Browsers

Palms

These appear in tree or shrub form.

Shapes are very distinctive with huge, spiky leaves.

Leaves are in clusters in shrubs, and at top of trunk in tree forms.

22
Wild date palm
Phoenix reclinata
Up to ± 6 m; evergreen
Habitat: Always found near water, on river banks & vleis
Trunk: Remnants of old leaves on trunk
Leaves: Arching with leaflets growing from central spine
Fruit: Date-like; yellow
Utilization: Browsed by elephant; birds, baboons & monkeys eat the fruit
• *Very easy to find*

A	E	I	M
B	F	J	N
C	G	K	O
D	H	L	P

23
Lala palm
Hyphaene natalensis
Up to 15 m; evergreen
Habitat: Not necessarily near water; clay soil
Trunk: Suckers from base grow in clumps
Leaves: Fan-like from central point
Fruit: Large (6 cm); hard, dark-brown, shiny
Utilization: Browsed by elephant
• *Very easy to find*

A	E	I	M
B	F	J	N
C	G	K	O
D	H	L	P

"Utilization" refers to the extent leaves and bark are eaten by browsers.

Trees that are easy to recognise by their shape

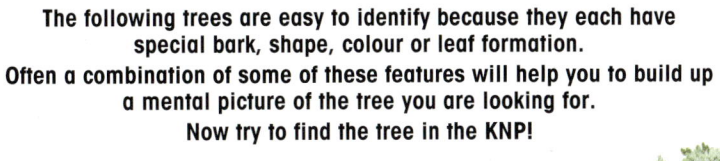

The following trees are easy to identify because they each have
special bark, shape, colour or leaf formation.
Often a combination of some of these features will help you to build up
a mental picture of the tree you are looking for.
Now try to find the tree in the KNP!

238
Apple-leaf / Rain tree
Lonchocarpus capassa

Up to 18 m (Riverine,
Alluvial); elsewhere up to
10 m; deciduous (leaves fall
in spring); "Rain tree" name
from fluid dripped by froth-
covered insects feeding on
tree in early summer
Trunk: Twisted
Crown: Branches wide-
spreading; bare;
sometimes carry
separated clumps
of crown
Leaves: Large; look faded
Flowers: Late summer;
pale mauve, dense,
drooping clusters
Fruit: Oct – Jan; green
to pale-brown clusters;
remain on trees
Utilization: Browsed by
elephants in dry periods
• **Very easy to find**

Clay soil

222
Tree wistaria
Bolusanthus speciosus

Up to 15 m, deciduous
Trunk: Slender, single or forked; few branches
Bark: Brown; deeply fissured
Crown: Whole tree drooping, soft, delicate appearance
Leaves: Long, light-green, glossy, drooping;
11-13 leaflets
Flowers: Sept – Oct; violet-blue drooping
grape-like bunches
Fruit: Feb – Mar; brown to black
Utilization: Browsed

360
Marula
Sclerocarya birrea, subsp. *caffra*

Up to 15 m; deciduous
Trunk: Straight, long, bare,
high-branching
Bark: Flakes off irregularly,
showing yellow-pink blocks
Crown: Wide-spread, round,
fairly dense; branchlets finger-like,
end abruptly
Flowers: Aug – Sep; mixed, dark
red-pink-white; separate (M) & (F) trees
Fruit: Jan – Feb; green berries;
ripen yellow
Utilization: Highly favoured
by all species; heavily browsed

Sandy soil

251
Green thorn/
Torchwood
Balanites maughamii

Up to 20 m; semi-deciduous
Trunk: Fluted, as if many trunks
have been joined together; tall,
straight, usually branching high up;
some side shoots often low down
Leaves: Look rigid, quite brittle;
consist of twin leaflets
Thorns: Forked, green
Fruit: May – Jul; like dates;
mature yellow-brown
Utilization: Regularly browsed;
particularly by elephant & giraffe;
fruit eaten by impala & baboon
• **Very easy to find**

551
Silver cluster-leaf
Terminalia sericea

Smallish; 8 m; deciduous
Habitat: Found in groups/lines
at the seepline, half way down
a slope
Trunk: Single, slender, low-branching
Bark: Grey; vertically ridged
Crown: Branches lateral, growing at right
angles to the trunk, (resembles a waiter
carrying a tray)
Leaves: In clusters, giving silvery
impression
Flowers: Oct – Nov;
dirty-white small spikes;
strong smelling
Fruit: Mar – Apr;
buff-green, then pinkish
Utilization: Seldom
browsed; fruit eaten
by insects

Trees that are easy to recognise in specific habitats

The following trees are easy to identify because each one
is common in a specific habitat.
Look at the pictures and read the descriptions,
which will help you to build up a mental picture of the tree.
Now try to find the tree in the Park!

Near permanent water

A	E	I	M
B	F	J	N
C	G	K	O
D	H	L	P

66
Sycamore fig
Ficus sycomorus,
subsp. *sycomorus*

Up to 20 m; mostly evergreen;
enormous and spreading
Trunk: Huge, thick & short-fluted
that often has low-down thick,
spreading branches
Bark: Very noticeable, yellowish,
skin-like
Fruit: All year; very visible
Utilization: Seldom browsed; fruit eaten
by birds & animals
• *Very easy to find*

301
Natal mahogany
Trichilia emetica

A	E	I	M
B	F	J	N
C	G	K	O
D	H	L	P

Up to 20 m; evergreen
Trunk: Thick & dark; low-branching
Crown: Very dense; round
Leaves: Big, shiny, dark-green
Flowers: Aug – Sep; green,
dense clusters
Fruit: Drooping clusters
Utilization: Seldom browsed;
fruit eaten by birds

341
Tamboti
Spirostachys africana

Up to 10 m; deciduous,
leaves turn red-brown
Bark: Divided into
small rectangles in
rows like rough
snake-skin
Crown: Quite dense;
very poisonous latex
in leaves, & even
smoke from braai
causes nausea
Flowers:
Aug – Sep
Fruit: Sep – Oct;
insects (pupae)
cause fruit to "hop"
on ground
Utilization: Bark
& leaves utilized
by black rhino
& porcupine

A	E	I	M
B	F	J	N
C	G	K	O
D	H	L	P

684
Matumi
Breonadia salicina

Up to 40 m;
evergreen;
smaller ones are
easy to
recognise
Leaves: Long,
fairly thick,
dark-green,
glossy; grow in groups
of four
Flowers: Nov – Mar; very small,
pale-yellow, densely packed in
round heads
Fruit: Jan – Feb; extremely
small; inconspicuous
Utilization: Not browsed
• *Very easy to find*

A	E	I	M
B	F	J	N
C	G	K	O
D	H	L	P

678
Sausage tree
Kigelia africana

Up to 20 m;
semi-deciduous to deciduous
Trunk: Very thick,
short, straight
Crown: Wide-
spreading,
dense, round
Leaves:
Shed late
winter –
early spring
Flowers: Jul –
Oct; distinctive
Fruit: Appear after
Aug, drop Mar – Apr;
sausages distinctive; not eaten
Utilization: Seldom browsed

A	E	I	M
B	F	J	N
C	G	K	O
D	H	L	P

"Utilization" refers to the extent leaves and bark are eaten by browsers.

202
Weeping boer-bean
Schotia brachypetala

Up to 12 m; deciduous
Bark : Rough, dark-grey; peels in small irregular blocks
Crown: Similar to Sausage tree (**678**) with smaller leaves that appear to grow downwards;
branches rigid, like fingers pointing downwards, giving quite dense umbrella shape
Flowers: Early spring; distinctive red
Fruit: Late summer; from pale-green to dark-brown; pale-yellow attachments to seeds
Utilization: Seldom browsed; young shoots only; pods eaten by birds

606
Jackal berry
Diospyros mespiliformis

Up to 20 m; deciduous; distinguishing feature is often size
Habitat: Riverine; sometimes on termitaria
Trunk: Single; divides into branches that appear almost as thick as trunk
Bark: Dark, almost black; can be confused with Tamboti (**341**)
Leaves: Dark-green; autumn dark-yellow
Fruit: Sep – Oct
Utilization: Seldom browsed; fruit eaten by birds & other animals (especially primates)

A	E	I	M
B	F	J	N
C	G	K	O
D	H	L	P

A	E	I	M
B	F	J	N
C	G	K	O
D	H	L	P

269
Mountain seringa
Kirkia wilmsii

Illustration as for White seringa (**267**) below, except trunk multi-stemmed & low-branching

Up to 10 m; deciduous
Crown: Roundish
Leaves: Same as White seringa
Flowers: Sep – Oct; masses of small yellow-green clusters
Fruit: Feb – Mar
Utilization: Limited, except by elephants

A	E	I	M
B	F	J	N
C	G	K	O
D	H	L	P

A	E	I	M
B	F	J	N
C	G	K	O
D	H	L	P

63
Large-leaved rock fig
Ficus abutilifolia

Up to 6 m; deciduous; distinctive, beautiful, branching, white roots that seem to hold rocks with long "syrupy" fingers
Trunk: Short, twisting, yellow-white
Fruit: All year; quite large, red when ripe
Utilization: Not browsed; fruit eaten by birds, primates & other game
• *Very easy to find*

A	E	I	M
B	F	J	N
C	G	K	O
D	H	L	P

267
White seringa
Kirkia acuminata

Up to 20 m; deciduous
Trunk: Long, straight, bare; thicker, older branches also bare
Crown: Spreads flat, silhouettes against the sky, on top of koppies
Leaves: Look like feather-dusters, crowded at the branch ends
Flowers: Oct – Dec; white clusters on long stalks
Fruit: Apr – May; visible through winter
Utilization: Browsed occasionally

Trees that are easy to recognise in specific habitats (continued)

207
Pod mahogany
Afzelia quansensis

Up to 20 m; deciduous
Trunk: Single, straight; sometimes huge
Bark: Pale grey-creamy brown, smoothish with circular ridges
Crown: Dense, spreading, sometimes wider than tree height
Leaves: Compound; leaflets shiny, waxy, feathery, wavy, drooping
Flowers: Oct – Nov; green, red-spotted, single petal
Fruit: Nov – Jan; most beautiful when open, showing white lining & red & black seeds
Utilization: Browsed by elephants

A	E	I	M
B	F	J	N
C	G	K	O
D	H	L	P

241
Nyala tree
Xanthocercis zambesiaca

Up to 30 m; evergreen to semi-deciduous
Trunk: Single, fluted; low-branching
Crown: Dense, spreading, rounded; spread often wider than height; branches drooping at ends
Flowers: Summer; small, white-creamy petals; fragrant
Fruit: Autumn – winter; oval, fleshy pulp
Utilization: Shade used, particularly by elephant, impala & nyala; pods used by many animals – birds, monkeys, baboons & herbivores

A	E	I	M
B	F	J	N
C	G	K	O
D	H	L	P

467
Baobab
Adansonia digitata

Up to 25 m; deciduous
Trunk: Huge, out of proportion to branches
Bark: Very smooth, skin-like
Crown: Branches gnarled & twisted like roots, as if tree has been turned upside down
Flowers: Oct – Nov; large, white
Fruit: Apr – May
Utilization: Flower pulp makes a refreshing drink; browsed by elephants; fruit eaten by baboons & monkeys
• **Very easy to find**

A	E	I	M
B	F	J	N
C	G	K	O
D	H	L	P

Common trees & shrubs with a rather untidy appearance

Always in shrub form

190
Sickle bush
Dichrostachys cinerea, subsp. *africana*

Up to 5 m; deciduous
Crown: Multi-stemmed; sometimes dense, round and untidy; lateral twigs modified, thorn-like, in pairs
Leaves: Similar to Acacias
Flowers: Sep – Feb; small, bottle-brush; orange & pink
Fruit: Summer/autumn; twisted, intertwined, sickle-shaped
Utilization: Heavily browsed; pods highly nutritious

595
Magic guarri
Euclea divinorum

6 m; evergreen
Crown: Multi-stemmed shrub/small tree; often in large stands
Leaves: Slender, grey-green; undulating edges; hard, thick
Flowers: Aug – Oct; Small dense groups in leaf axils; (M) & (F) separate
Fruit: Apr – May; Small, very hard, round, dull red-brown
Utilization: Very seldom browsed

A	E	I	M
B	F	J	N
C	G	K	O
D	H	L	P

A	E	I	M
B	F	J	N
C	G	K	O
D	H	L	P

621
Transvaal mustard tree
Salvadora angustifolia,
subsp. *australis*
Up to 7 m; evergreen
Crown: Sparse, spreading, twiggy;
lower branches on the ground;
stem short, crooked
Leaves: Simple; buff-green;
in pairs; brittle; salty taste
Flowers: Aug; inconspicuous,
greenish-yellow
Fruit: Nov – Dec; small
Utilization: Important food plant
for browsers; edible fruit

A	E	I	M
B	F	J	N
C	G	K	O
D	H	L	P

458, 459.1, 459.2, 460, 463.1, 463.2
Raisin bush
Grewia species

A number of similar species occur; this illustration represents
the numbers above; in right habitat occur in large numbers

Shrubs 2-5 m; deciduous
Crown: Multi-stemmed; branches thin, wavy; in some species
rectangular in cross-section (not round)
Leaves: Silvery tinge, whiter underside in some species
Flowers: Summer; mainly yellow
Fruit: Smallish, some single & round, others with 4 fused fruits
(cross-berries); high sugar & protein content
Utilization: Browsed by a variety of game; fruit eaten by birds & animals

Shrub or tree form

Geology, land-shape and rainfall determine the size of certain trees.
In the KNP, these trees, occur in large and small forms.

A	E	I	M
B	F	J	N
C	G	K	O
D	H	L	P

447
Buffalo thorn
Ziziphus mucronata, subsp. *mucronata*
Afrikaans name: "Wag 'n bietjie"
(Wait-a-bit thorn)
Up to 9 m; deciduous
Crown: Branchlets very
noticeable zigzags
Leaves: Thin, curling in
on upper surface; very
glossy, yellow-green
to dark-green
Thorns: In pairs; 1 straight,
1 curved backwards
Flowers: Oct – Feb
Fruit: Jan – Jul; berries
yellow-reddish / brown
Utilization: Browsed
extensively; edible fruit

A	E	I	M
B	F	J	N
C	G	K	O
D	H	L	P

198
Mopane
Colophospermum mopane
From multi-stemmed shrub (2 m)
to tree (18 m); deciduous
Habitat: Both tree & shrub unmistakable because
they dominate particular Ecozones
Leaves: Jul – Aug leaves turn yellowish to pale-brown;
look like a butterfly with open wings
Flowers: Dec – Jan; small, yellowish-green, inconspicuous
Fruit: Apr – May; flat, semi-circular in shape;
pale-brown; single-seeded
Utilization: Heavily browsed, especially by elephant
• **Very easy to find**

237
Round-leafed teak
Pterocarpus rotundifolius, subsp. *rotundifolius*
Up to 15 m; deciduous
Shrubs occur in massed clumps;
single-stemmed trees rare
Leaves: Compound; large,
round, glossy, dark-green
Flowers: Nov – Dec or
later; yellow clusters
Pods: Ripen late
summer – autumn
Utilization: Browsed,
especially
by elephant

A	E	I	M
B	F	J	N
C	G	K	O
D	H	L	P

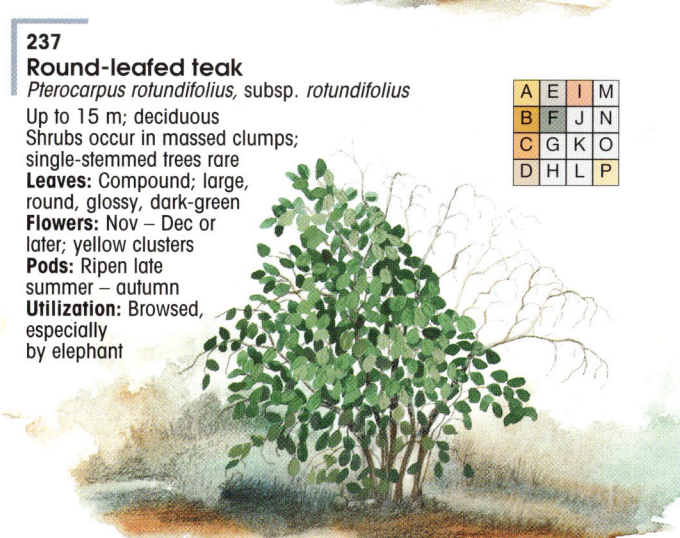

550
Thorny cluster-leaf
Terminalia prunioides
Shrub to small tree; 9 m;
deciduous
Crown: Sparse with loose
branches; side twigs end in
thorn-like protrusions
Leaves: Clustered spirally
around branchlets
Flowers: Sep – Feb
Fruit: Feb – May; often more
than once in a season
Utilization: Poorly browsed

A	E	I	M
B	F	J	N
C	G	K	O
D	H	L	P

"Utilization" means to what extent leaves and bark are eaten by browsers.

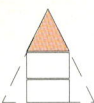

ANIMALS

Most animals spend a great deal of their waking hours gathering sufficient food for survival for themselves and often for their young too. When looking for animals, look near their food source.

All animals (mammals, birds, reptiles and insects) can be classified according to their method of feeding into one of the following categories. They are either insectivorous (eating insects), herbivorous (eating vegetable matter), carnivorous (eating meat) or omnivorous (eating all forms of food).

Grazers, like zebra, wildebeest and buffalo, are animals of the grassland. They are hunted by lion and cheetah who stalk, run and pounce.

Grazing animals, in large herds and on open plains, escape from predators through their speed.

There is also protection simply in the number of individuals who are alert... and available to be taken! The principle of group protection also applies to seed-eating birds.

Browsers, like bushbuck, steenbok, duiker and nyala are found in the bushier areas of the Kruger National Park.

These buck are hunted by leopards, who hide, well camouflaged, and pounce suddenly. In woody, bushy areas, both the predator's and the antelope's camouflage tends to be spots or soft stripy lines to conceal them among the leaves and branches.

Here you will also find impala, who browse **and** graze, depending on the availability of food.

In Nature, survival hinges on an effective chain of connecting elements. A rule we apply to our products and services too.

Water, like land, has an infinite, interdependent number of food cycles.

Frogs are generally insectivorous, while terrapins are one of the scavengers that keep the water clean.

Animals on the plains have camouflage
to blur the outlines between individuals.
This makes the herd appear as a solid mass,
which reduces the chance of a lion picking
out a single individual.

Try half closing your eyes as you look at a herd
of zebra, and see the effect!

The cycles created by
the need for food are endless.
The eggs of the guinea fowl are food
for the leguaan, while he too is a meal
for the martial eagle.
Tiny canaries eat grass seeds. This grass also
feeds large waterbuck and hides wild dogs.

Dung beetles carry animal dung below
the surface to fertilise the soil. It is essential
that nutrients originally derived from plants
(when eaten by animals) are recycled back into
the soil as food for the vegetation.

To help you to become familiar with
as many common species as possible,
and as fast as possible, the following pages
are laid out in such a way that you can
easily compare species that are similar.

**The following pages describe the mammals, birds, reptiles and
insects that visitors are most likely to see in the Kruger National Park.**

Mammals

These pages are designed to help you to look for animals in the right places and to identify them when you see them. To help you recognise the main differences between similar animals, they have been grouped together.

To help you judge the size of the mammals, they are recorded as follows:
Height: Ground to shoulder in centimetres or metres
Length: Tip of nose – tip of tail in centimetres or metres
Weight: In grams or kilograms
(M) = Male; (F) = Female

Many species of animals lay eggs, but all mammals give birth to young which are milk-fed by the mother. This leads to mother-child bonding, with the mother protecting the young. Generally, therefore, mammals give birth to fewer young than insects or reptiles and, to ensure their survival, they take care of them until they are mature enough to fend for themselves.

Small mammals

There are many species of interesting small mammals in the KNP. They live in every kind of habitat from underground to high in the branches. They eat every type of living material from plants to insects and meat.

Diurnal

You can mostly see these animals during the day

Chacma baboon
(M) 1,4 m, (F) 1,1 m (length);
(M) 30 kg, (F) 16 kg
Habitat: Savannah; mountains
Grouping: Gregarious; up to 50 in a troop
Breeding: All year, mainly in summer; 1, rarely 2 young
Diet: Omnivorous; berries; fruit; seeds; buds; eggs of birds; insects

Vervet monkey
1 m (length); 5 kg
Habitat: Riverine vegetation & bushy areas; near permanent water
Grouping: Gregarious; troops up to 20
Breeding: Mostly Dec – Feb; 1, rarely 2 young
Diet: Fruit; flowers; seed pods; insects; young birds; eggs

Tree squirrel
35 cm (length); 190 g
Habitat: Throughout the KNP; especially tree savannah
Grouping: Solitary or pairs
Breeding: All year; 2-3 young
Diet: Fruit seeds; shoots; roots; insects

Dwarf mongoose
38 cm (length); 260 g
Habitat: Open savannah with termitaria or other hiding places
Grouping: Gregarious; groups of 20 or more
Breeding: Summer months; 2-4 young
Diet: Insects; beetles & their larvae; snakes; snails; birds' eggs

Banded mongoose
55 cm (length); 1,3 kg
Habitat: Closed savannah in thickets; rocky outcrops
Grouping: Gregarious; packs up to 30 or more
Breeding: Oct – Feb; 2-6 young
Diet: Millipedes; centipedes; spiders; insects; termites; carrion; snakes; wild fruit

Nocturnal

You can mostly see these animals at dawn and dusk

Lesser bushbaby
40 cm (length); 150 g
Habitat: Savannah, especially Acacia
Grouping: Singly, or small family groups
Breeding: Summer; 2-3 young
Diet: Insects; wild berries; flowers

Thick-tailed bushbaby
60 cm (length); 1,1 kg
Habitat: Live in trees; well-wooded areas
Grouping: Solitary; pairs or small family groups
Breeding: First 3 weeks Nov; 2, occasionally 3 young
Diet: Omnivorous; berries; fruits; insects; leafy shoots; gum; small animals; birds & birds' eggs

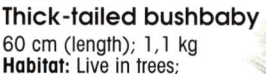

Porcupine
76 cm (length); 14 kg
Habitat: Throughout the KNP; favour broken country
Grouping: Solitary or pairs
Breeding: Autumn or early winter; 1-3 young
Diet: Roots; bulbs; wild fruit

Scrub hare
55 cm (length); 2 kg
Habitat: Open savannah; good grass cover
Grouping: Single; occasionally pairs
Breeding: All year; 1-3 young
Diet: Grass

Antbear (Aardvark)
1,6 m (length); 52 kg
Habitat: Throughout the KNP
Grouping: Usually solitary
Breeding: Late winter, early spring; 1 young
Diet: Insectivorous

Look out for fascinating bats! You can see them during the day sleeping in large trees, under bridges, in crevices or flying around camps in the evening.

Herbivores

Browsers eat bark, leaves, buds, fruit, pods and flowers that are found in bushy areas of the KNP. Grazers eat grass as their main diet. A few animals, like impala and elephant, both graze and browse. Some herbivores depend on water every day and are found near major rivers and dams; others, like klipspringer, can survive for long periods using only the liquid from plants.

Grazers

A	E	I	M
B	F	J	N
C	G	K	O
D	H	L	P

Buffalo
1,6 m (height); 750 kg
Habitat: Open savannah; permanent water supply
Grouping: Gregarious, herds up to 500; bulls often solitary
Breeding: Mar – May; 1 calf
Diet: Grazers; tall, coarse grass

African elephant
2,8 m (height); (M) 5 750 kg, (F) 3 800 kg
Habitat: Closed savannah
Grouping: Family herds led by matriarch; mature bulls solitary or in separate groups
Breeding: All year; 1 calf
Diet: Large quantities of grass when available; shoots; roots; bark; leaves; fruits

A	E	I	M
B	F	J	N
C	G	K	O
D	H	L	P

Burchell's zebra
1,3 m (height); 230 kg
Habitat: Open savannah; regular water supply
Grouping: Gregarious, family groups
Breeding: Oct – Mar (with peak Dec – Feb); 1 foal
Diet: Grazers; particularly taller grass

A	E	I	M
B	F	J	N
C	G	K	O
D	H	L	P

Giraffe
3,3 m (height); 1 200 kg
Habitat: Closed savannah; daily water not essential
Breeding: All year; 1 calf (rarely 2)
Diet: Browsers, particularly Acacia leaves

A	E	I	M
B	F	J	N
C	G	K	O
D	H	L	P

Blue wildebeest
(M) 1,5 m, (F) 1,35 m (height); (M) 250 kg, (F) 180 kg
Habitat: Open plains; short grass
Grouping: Highly gregarious; can form large herds; normally 2-15
Breeding: End Nov – Jan; 1 calf
Diet: Grazers; primarily short grass

A	E	I	M
B	F	J	N
C	G	K	O
D	H	L	P

Browsers

A	E	I	M
B	F	J	N
C	G	K	O
D	H	L	P

Hippopotamus
1,5 m (height); 1 500 kg
Habitat: Permanent pools; rivers with good grass cover on the banks; during day in water or resting on river-banks; graze on land at night
Grouping: Gregarious; herds about 15, with dominant bull
Breeding: All year (with summer peak); 1 calf
Diet: Grazers

Black rhino
1,6 m (height); 800-1100 kg
Pointed lip, head held high for browsing
Habitat: Closed savannah; prefer thickets
Grouping: Solitary; (M) territorial; (F) with offspring up to 3 years old
Breeding: All year, especially in summer; 1 calf
Diet: Browsers; twigs; leaves; forbs

A	E	I	M
B	F	J	N
C	G	K	O
D	H	L	P

Warthog
(M) 70 cm, (F) 60 cm (height); (M) 80 kg, (F) 55 kg
Habitat: Open savannah; with short grass
Grouping: Family groups
Breeding: Oct – Dec; 3-4 piglets
Diet: Mixed feeder; roots; tubers; fruit; short grass

White rhino
1,8 m (height); (M) 2 300 kg, (F) 1 600 kg
Square lip, head hangs low for grazing
Habitat: Flat open plains; short grass; permanent water
Grouping: Territorial; small family groups
Breeding: All year; 1 calf (3-year intervals)
Diet: Grazers; fond of Guinea grass
N.B. There is no colour difference between white and black rhinos.

A	E	I	M
B	F	J	N
C	G	K	O
D	H	L	P

Sally MacLarty

67

Herbivores (continued)

A	E	I	M
B	F	J	N
C	G	K	O
D	H	L	P

Impala
(M) 91 cm, (F) 85 cm (height);
(M) 65 kg, (F) 45 kg
Habitat: Near permanent water where veld is intensely grazed
Grouping: Herds 20-400; led by dominant ram; (M) join bachelor herds at 2 yrs old
Breeding: Mid Nov – mid Jan; 1 lamb annually
Diet: Browsers & grazers; particularly grass in disturbed areas

Browsers

A	E	I	M
B	F	J	N
C	G	K	O
D	H	L	P

Nyala
(M) 1,1 m, (F) 1 m (height);
(M) 110 kg, (F) 75 kg
Habitat: Riverine bush common along Luvuvhu River
Grouping: Groups of 2-5
Breeding: Sep – Mar; 1 lamb
Diet: Mainly browsers; eat more grass than kudu

Kudu

(M) 1,4 m, (F) 1,25 m (height);
(M) 200-260 kg, (F) 150 kg
Habitat: Closed savannah; hilly terrain
Grouping: Family groups up to 12
Breeding: Mar – Apr; 1 calf
Diet: Mainly browsers

A	E	I	M
B	F	J	N
C	G	K	O
D	H	L	P

Mountain reedbuck
70-75 cm (height); (M) 30 kg, (F) 28 kg
Habitat: Mountainous areas with good grass cover; especially in the south west of the KNP
Grouping: Herds of 3-6, up to 15; active early morning and late afternoon
Breeding: Sep – Mar; 1 calf
Diet: Grazers; often seen on burnt areas after rains

A	E	I	M
B	F	J	N
C	G	K	O
D	H	L	P

Grazers

A	E	I	M
B	F	J	N
C	G	K	O
D	H	L	P

Common reedbuck
(M) 90 cm, (F) 80 cm (height);
(M) 80 kg, (F) 70 kg
Habitat: Near water, with stands of tall grass or reedbeds
Grouping: Pairs or family groups
Breeding: Dec – May; 1 lamb
Diet: Grazers; mainly longer grass

Bushbuck
70-80 cm (height); (M) 60 kg, (F) 35 kg
Habitat: Riverine thickets; dense undergrowth
Grouping: Solitary, small groups
Breeding: Oct – Nov; 1 lamb
Diet: Mainly browsers

A	E	I	M
B	F	J	N
C	G	K	O
D	H	L	P

Klipspringer
60 cm (height);
(M) 11 kg, (F) 13 kg
Habitat: Rocky outcrops
Grouping: Territorial; pairs; small family groups
Breeding: All year; 1 lamb
Diet: Browsers; fruits; only drink water when available

A	E	I	M
B	F	J	N
C	G	K	O
D	H	L	P

Grazers

Waterbuck
(M) 1,7 m, (F) 1,3 m (height);
(M) 260 kg, (F) 230 kg
Habitat: Close to water; more open areas; tall to medium grass; hilly areas
Grouping: Herds of 10-30
Breeding: All year; peak Jan – Mar; 1 calf
Diet: Grazers

Sable antelope
1,35 m (height);
(M) 250 kg, (F) 210 kg
Habitat: Open savannah with tall grass; prefer granitic areas
Grouping: Few individuals; herds up to 40
Breeding: Feb – Mar; 1 calf
Diet: Mainly grazers; preferably grass taller than 8 cm

Roan antelope
(M) 1,55 m, (F) 1,45 m (height);
(M) 280 kg, (F) 250 kg
Habitat: Open savannah with tall grass; especially north of Letaba River
Grouping: Herds up to 12
Breeding: All year; 1 calf
Diet: Grazers; particularly medium-tall grass

Eland
(M) 1,7 m, (F) 1,5 m (height);
(M) 700 kg, (F) 450 kg
Largest Southern African antelope
Habitat: Open savannah; especially north of Olifants River
Grouping: Small family groups; sometimes join together in larger herds
Breeding: All year, peak Sep – Nov; 1 calf
Diet: Browsers

Tsessebe
1,2 m (height);
(M) 140 kg, (F) 120 kg
Habitat: Open savannah especially north of Letaba River
Grouping: Small herds of 4-10
Breeding: Mid Sep – early Nov; 1 calf
Diet: Grazers; medium-height grass; avoid over-grazed areas

Lichtenstein's hartebeest
1,25 m (height);
170-180 kg
Habitat: Open savannah; far north; open woodlands
Grouping: Territorial males; small herds up to 10
Breeding: Peak Sep; 1 calf
Diet: Grazers

Browsers

Common duiker
(M) 50 cm, (F) 52 cm (height);
(M) 18 kg, (F) 20 kg
Habitat: Thickets along water courses
Grouping: Solitary or pairs; usually secretive
Breeding: All year; 1 lamb
Diet: Mainly browsers; also grass & fruits

Steenbok
50-60 cm (height);
± 11 kg
Habitat: Plains in open savannah with short to medium-height grass
Grouping: Territorial; solitary; pairs briefly for mating
Breeding: All year; 1 lamb
Diet: Mainly browsers

Sharpe's grysbok
50 cm (height); 8 kg
Habitat: Broken & hilly country; along eastern watercourses; prefer areas with low vegetation
Grouping: Solitary
Breeding: All year; 1 lamb
Diet: Mainly browsers

MICHAEL THAYER

69

Carnivores

These pages describe the meat-eaters that you are most likely to see and where, and how you will find them! Those which look alike have been grouped together.

Carnivores control the population numbers of herbivores. By selecting weaker animals as prey, survival of the fittest leads to healthy animals of every kind.

Further reading:
Field Guide to the Mammals of the Kruger National Park
– U de V Pienaar, S C J Joubert, A Hall-Martin, G de Graaff, I L Rautenbach
Field Guide to the Mammals of Southern Africa
– Chris & Tilde Stuart
Animals of the Kruger National Park
– G de Graaff

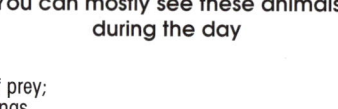

Diurnal
You can mostly see these animals during the day

Wild dog
68 cm (height); 24-30 kg
Hunt late afternoon, evening
Habitat: Adequate water; abundance of prey; areas where there are few lions or hyaenas
Grouping: Highly gregarious; packs up to 40
Breeding: May – Jul; dry winter; 2-8 pups
Diet: Small to large mammals, depending on size of pack

Cheetah
75 cm (height);
(M) 50 kg, (F) 40 kg
Habitat: Open plains; savannah woodland
Grouping: Solitary, pair for mating
Breeding: All year; 2-4 cubs
Diet: Medium-small antelope; warthog; young of large mammals

Nocturnal
You can mostly see these animals at dawn and dusk

Leopard
70 cm (height);
60-80 kg
Habitat: Dense riverine bush or forest; mountains
Grouping: Solitary, except (F) with young
Breeding: All year; 2-3 cubs
Diet: Insects; fish; reptiles; baboon; impala

Side-striped jackal
38 cm (height); 8-10 kg
Habitat: Typical savannah woodlands
Grouping: Solitary in the day; but pair up before sunset
Breeding: Sep – Nov; 2-6 pups
Diet: Carrion; rodents; insects; beetles; termites; reptiles; fruits

Black-backed jackal
38 cm (height); 7-8 kg
Habitat: Relatively dry conditions; savannah & woodlands
Grouping: Singly, pairs or parties
Breeding: Spring & summer; 4-9 pups
Diet: Carrion; small mammals; rodents; ground-nesting birds; reptiles; insects

Hyaena
70-80 cm (height); 65-70 kg
Habitat: Savannah plains
Grouping: Clans of between 5 & 20
Breeding: All year; 2-3 pups
Diet: Predator & scavenger; bones

Clawless otter
1.3 m (length); 13 kg
Habitat: Quiet backwaters; thick vegetation alongside water
Grouping: Solitary or in pairs
Breeding: Mar – Apr; 2-3 pups
Diet: Crabs; molluscs; fish; aquatic birds; rodents; frogs

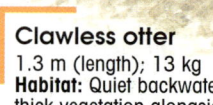

Lion
1 m (height); (M) 180-230 kg, (F) 113-160 kg
Habitat: Very wide range depending on food supply
Grouping: Highly social; small family prides to big groups
Breeding: All year; 2-3 cubs
Diet: Medium-large hoofed animals; carrion
N.B. You can see lions during the day, at dusk & at dawn.

A	E	I	M
B	F	J	N
C	G	K	O
D	H	L	P

Serval
50 cm (height); 10-13 kg
Habitat: Reedbeds; tall grass; low bush
Grouping: Pairs or single
Breeding: Summer; 2-4 kittens
Diet: Rodents; reptiles; insects; birds; frogs; wild fruits

A	E	I	M
B	F	J	N
C	G	K	O
D	H	L	P

Nocturnal
You can mostly see these animals at dawn and dusk

A	E	I	M
B	F	J	N
C	G	K	O
D	H	L	P

Caracal
40 cm (height);
(M) 13 kg, (F) 10 kg
Habitat: Thick bush & rocky outcrops
Grouping: Solitary; pair briefly for mating
Breeding: In summer months; 2-4 cubs
Diet: Birds; small mammals; rodents

A	E	I	M
B	F	J	N
C	G	K	O
D	H	L	P

Spotted genet
95 cm (length); ±2 kg
Both Large-spotted and Small-spotted genets are found in the KNP
Habitat: Widespread; especially savannah regions with high rainfall
Grouping: Mainly solitary
Breeding: Wet summer months; 2-3 kittens
Diet: Small & large mammals

Civet
1,3 m (length); 10 kg
Habitat: Well-watered grassland
Grouping: Generally solitary
Breeding: Wet summer months; 2-3 cubs
Diet: Omnivorous; insects; wild fruit; birds; rodents; fish

A	E	I	M
B	F	J	N
C	G	K	O
D	H	L	P

Striped polecat
62 cm (length); (M) 95 g, (F) 70 g
Habitat: Holes in the ground; rocky crevices; dense bush
Grouping: Singly, pairs or mothers with young
Breeding: Oct – Nov; 1-3 kittens
Diet: Rodents; reptiles; insects; birds; frogs; snakes

A	E	I	M
B	F	J	N
C	G	K	O
D	H	L	P

A	E	I	M
B	F	J	N
C	G	K	O
D	H	L	P

African wild cat
38 cm (height); 4-5 kg
Habitat: Wide spread; tall grass & thick bush
Grouping: Solitary, but may hunt in pairs
Breeding: Summer months; litter up to 5 kittens
Diet: Rodents; birds; reptiles; insects; hares; fruit

Honey badger
95 cm (length); 12 kg
Habitat: Very wide spread
Grouping: Generally solitary
Breeding: Spring – summer; 2 pups
Diet: Reptiles; insects; larvae of dung beetles; eggs; ground birds; wild fruits; honey

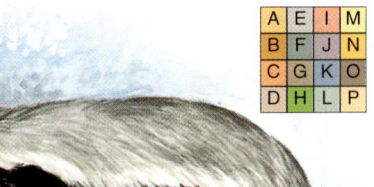

A	E	I	M
B	F	J	N
C	G	K	O
D	H	L	P

Sally MacLarty

Birds

Nearly 500 species of birds have been identified in the Kruger National Park.

You will add interest to your hour, and your day, by spotting a bird that you have never seen before!

This list contains 90 of the more common birds that you are likely to see and identify, most of the year round.

Birds are more easily identified if you know where to find them. Specific species live in a particular area or habitat. To help you look, the following pages show groupings of birds in their most likely habitats, e.g. African fish eagles and Green pigeons are usually found in trees near permanent water, such as rivers or large dams.

To see birds, large mammals and reptiles in their natural environment you need to visit a wildlife reserve. Smaller birds are the one species that you can carry on watching after leaving the KNP. Start by learning a few of the more colourful and easy-to-spot species and you will find pleasure for years to come, wherever you are.

All birds listed below are:

❏ resident & breed locally
❏ solitary or in pairs
(unless otherwise stated)
❏ numbered with a "Roberts" number

Bird sizes are measured:

❏ from the beak-tip to the tail-tip,
or toe-tip (whichever is longer)

(M) = Male; (F) = Female

Further reading:
Field Guide to the Birds of the Kruger National Park
– Ian Sinclair & Ian Whyte
Roberts' Birds of Southern Africa
– Gordon Lindsay MacLean
Birds of the Kruger National Park
– Kenneth Newman

Birds in dry bushveld

Hunting from a perch

447
Lilacbreasted roller
36 cm
Breeding: Characteristic rolling flight in the breeding season (from which name stems)
Diet: Insects; small snakes; lizards; rodents

735
Longtailed shrike
45 cm
Long tails are jerked while birds call from prominent perch
Grouping: Sociable small groups; 3-10 birds
Diet: Insects; small reptiles

435
Brownhooded kingfisher
23 cm
Bush kingfisher; perch conspicuously to search for prey; not known to eat fish in the KNP
Breeding: Excavate nests out of sandbanks; make a chamber at the end of a 1 m tunnel
Diet: Mostly insects; also invertebrates

541
Forktailed drongo
24 cm
Very common; aggressive; mob larger raptors that enter territory; follow antelope to catch flushed insects; often seen perched prominently in trees
Diet: Mainly insects

433
Woodland kingfisher
23 cm
Summer migrant; has very characteristic call *"krit-trrrrrr"*, heard in summer months
Habitat: Lives in woodland (as name suggests), not necessarily near water
Diet: Mainly insects; also lizards, snakes, frogs

With antelope

772
Redbilled oxpecker
21 cm
Most common oxpecker in the KNP; warn host animals by flying away noisily when sensing danger
Grouping: Small groups 2-6
Diet: Mostly ticks; also horseflies, other insects

756
Whitecrowned shrike
24 cm
Habitat: Perch conspicuously
Grouping: Small scattered groups; up to 12 birds
Diet: Insects

444
Little bee-eater
17 cm
Stalk flying insects by fast flight from perch; use same perch day after day
Grouping: Solitary or pairs by day; small groups roosting in branches at night
Diet: Flying insects

You will get more enjoyment from bird watching if you use a pair of binoculars.

146
Bateleur
55-70 cm
Very conspicuous raptor due to short tail & colour of face & feet; often seen flying with side-to-side, tight-rope walker flight action
Diet: Carrion; birds; mammals up to 4 kg

(M)
(F)

A	E	I	M
B	F	J	N
C	G	K	O
D	H	L	P

527
Lesser striped swallow
16 cm
More common in summer; striped breasts make them easy to identify
Habitat: Near bridges, road culverts & buildings
Grouping: Pairs; small flocks
Diet: Flying insects

A	E	I	M
B	F	J	N
C	G	K	O
D	H	L	P

126
Yellowbilled kite
55 cm
Summer breeding migrant; scavenge actively, especially on roads, at camps & picnic sites; very common where termites emerge
Diet: Carrion; insects; crustaceans; small mammals; reptiles

A	E	I	M
B	F	J	N
C	G	K	O
D	H	L	P

In the sky

A	E	I	M
B	F	J	N
C	G	K	O
D	H	L	P

417
Little swift
14 cm
Vocal, particularly in the evenings; feed, drink & gather nesting material while flying
Grouping: Highly gregarious; big flocks mix with other swifts & swallows
Diet: Insects & spiders

A	E	I	M
B	F	J	N
C	G	K	O
D	H	L	P

142
Brown snake eagle
75 cm
Legs not feathered, as need heavy scales for protection against snake bites
Grouping: Usually solitary
Diet: Snakes up to 3 m long; monitors; smaller lizards

A	E	I	M
B	F	J	N
C	G	K	O
D	H	L	P

89
Marabou stork
1,5 m
These birds are scavengers; only occur where enough carrion is available, therefore seldom seen outside KNP
Grouping: Usually gregarious
Diet: Mostly carrion; also birds & fish when large numbers are readily available

A	E	I	M
B	F	J	N
C	G	K	O
D	H	L	P

140
Martial eagle
80 cm
Largest eagle in Africa; hunt on the wing, or from a perch; very large powerful talons to grasp prey
Diet: Larger birds; small mammals (duiker size); reptiles, especially monitors

124
Lappetfaced vulture
1 m
Biggest vulture; dominant over other vultures at carcass, but do not necessarily compete with them
Diet: Carrion, including tough skin & ligaments; also kill small mammals; barbel

A	E	I	M
B	F	J	N
C	G	K	O
D	H	L	P

123
Whitebacked vulture
94 cm
Most common vulture; like most vultures have excellent eyesight to find food; occur in large numbers at kills
Grouping: Gregarious, breed in trees in loose colonies
Diet: Carrion (often chase smaller vultures off carrion)

A	E	I	M
B	F	J	N
C	G	K	O
D	H	L	P

In large trees

373
Grey lourie
49 cm
Called "*go away bird*"
because of call
Grouping: Pairs; small parties
Diet: Fruit; flower-buds;
insects; leaves; seeds

A	E	I	M
B	F	J	N
C	G	K	O
D	H	L	P

464
Blackcollared barbet
20 cm
(M) & (F) call in
ringing duet perched
prominently on tree
Grouping: Solitary or pairs;
small groups
Breeding: Nest is a hole,
often in underside of dead branch
Diet: Fruit; insects

A	E	I	M
B	F	J	N
C	G	K	O
D	H	L	P

740
Puffback
18 cm
In display (M) puffs up
back feathers giving it a rounder
shape; hence the Afrikaans name
"sneeubal" (snowball); more
visible than other bush shrikes
Diet: Insects

A	E	I	M
B	F	J	N
C	G	K	O
D	H	L	P

568
Blackeyed bulbul
22 cm
Very common; highly
vocal & restless
Grouping: Pairs;
loose groups
Diet: Fruit; nectar;
insects; small lizards

A	E	I	M
B	F	J	N
C	G	K	O
D	H	L	P

A	E	I	M
B	F	J	N
C	G	K	O
D	H	L	P

398
Pearlspotted owl
19 cm
Often hunt by day;
hunt by dropping onto prey;
can catch bats in flight
Breeding: Breed in old
barbet holes
Diet: Mostly insects; small
mammals; birds; amphibians

A	E	I	M
B	F	J	N
C	G	K	O
D	H	L	P

545
Blackheaded oriole
25 cm
Call very distinctive; liquid
piping notes often heard early
in the morning
Grouping: Solitary or pairs;
loose groups at food source
Diet: Insects; fruit; nectar

426
Redfaced mousebird
34 cm
Resemble mice as they
clamber through the trees
Grouping: Gregarious;
in small groups,
up to 8 birds
Diet: Mainly fruit;
flowers; nectar

A	E	I	M
B	F	J	N
C	G	K	O
D	H	L	P

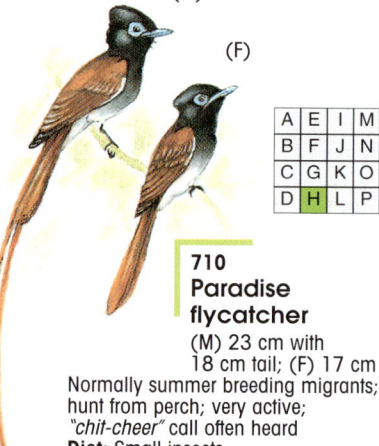

(M)

(F)

A	E	I	M
B	F	J	N
C	G	K	O
D	H	L	P

710
Paradise flycatcher
(M) 23 cm with
18 cm tail; (F) 17 cm
Normally summer breeding migrants;
hunt from perch; very active;
"*chit-cheer*" call often heard
Diet: Small insects

A	E	I	M
B	F	J	N
C	G	K	O
D	H	L	P

354
Cape turtle dove
28 cm
Very common; smallest and palest
of ring neck doves; call likened to
"*work harder – work harder*"
Grouping: Groups & mixed
parties; large numbers at
food source
Diet: Seeds; insects;
winged termites

A	E	I	M
B	F	J	N
C	G	K	O
D	H	L	P

353
Mourning dove
30 cm
Call is a soft resonant
"*ku-kur-rrr*"; red skin around eye
distinguishes it from other doves
Habitat: Common at Letaba
Camp; can be very tame
Grouping: In pairs but flocks
gather at food sources
Diet: Seed & grain

Against tree trunks

A	E	I	M
B	F	J	N
C	G	K	O
D	H	L	P

452
Redbilled woodhoopoe
34 cm
Loud cackling call likened to a
group of women laughing; fly from
tree to tree in noisy group; use long
bills to probe for insects beneath
bark or in holes in wood
Habitat: Prefer open Acacia to
dense woodland
Grouping: Gregarious groups of 2-16
Diet: Insects; millipedes; lizards; nectar

A	E	I	M
B	F	J	N
C	G	K	O
D	H	L	P

486
Cardinal woodpecker
15 cm
Small woodpecker; only (M)
has red on head; tap quietly
but rapidly, often in small
trees; insert barbed tongue
to withdraw insects
Diet: Beetle larvae
& other insects

(M)

(M)

A	E	I	M
B	F	J	N
C	G	K	O
D	H	L	P

483
Goldentailed woodpecker
22 cm
(F) has less red on head;
loud, echoing tap is a form
of communication
Diet: Ants & larvae; other insects

1
Ostrich
2 m
World's largest bird; prefer short grass plains, therefore mostly found in eastern half of the KNP, north of Letaba River
Grouping: Family groups
Diet: Mainly vegetarian; grass; berries; seeds

(M)

230
Kori bustard
(M) 1,2-1,5 m, (F) 1,0-1,2 m
World's heaviest flying bird; reluctant flyer, run before take off; occur in open plains, more often seen in eastern side of the KNP
Diet: Locusts; grasshoppers; Acacia gum; seeds; lizards; small rodents

A	E	I	M
B	F	J	N
C	G	K	O
D	H	L	P

463
Ground hornbill
1,1 m
Common throughout the KNP; have a loud resounding booming call, often heard early in the morning; on the endangered species list; mainly terrestrial, but sleep in trees
Grouping: Family groups 4-10
Diet: Entirely carnivorous; reptiles; tortoises; small mammals; snails; insects

A	E	I	M
B	F	J	N
C	G	K	O
D	H	L	P

A	E	I	M
B	F	J	N
C	G	K	O
D	H	L	P

237
Redcrested korhaan
50 cm
Well-camouflaged in long grass; red crest is not conspicuous, except in display
Breeding: In breeding season (M) flies vertically up 10-30 m, then folds wings & falls back to ground; polygamous
Diet: Arthropods; seeds; fruit; gum

(M)

203
Helmeted guineafowl
57 cm
Reddish-brown 'helmet' on top of head is a projection of bone; often walk in single file to water
Grouping: Highly gregarious when not breeding; flocks of hundreds of birds
Diet: Ants; termites; arthropods; tubers

196
Natal francolin
36 cm
Identified by black eye, red bill & legs
Habitat: Rocky areas near water
Grouping: Pairs; groups up to 10 birds
Diet: Molluscs; insects; roots; bulbs; fruit; seeds

A	E	I	M
B	F	J	N
C	G	K	O
D	H	L	P

189
Crested francolin
32 cm
Identified by black eye & bill, red legs; tail is often cocked like that of a bantam chicken; very noisy at dawn & dusk
Grouping: Pairs; small groups
Diet: Bulbs; seeds; berries; insects; molluscs

A	E	I	M
B	F	J	N
C	G	K	O
D	H	L	P

A	E	I	M
B	F	J	N
C	G	K	O
D	H	L	P

255
Crowned plover
30 cm
Occur throughout the KNP on heavily grazed areas; call well-known *"keefeeet"* when flying up; only plover to breed in loose colonies, probably for protection
Grouping: Gregarious; outside of breeding season up to 40 in group
Diet: Variety of insects & their larvae

199
Swainson's francolin
(M) 38 cm, (F) 33 cm
Identified by red face & throat, brown legs
Habitat: Grassland & areas not far from water
Grouping: Solitary or pairs; small groups
Diet: Seeds; berries; shoots; roots; bulbs; insects; molluscs

A	E	I	M
B	F	J	N
C	G	K	O
D	H	L	P

A	E	I	M
B	F	J	N
C	G	K	O
D	H	L	P

347
Doublebanded sandgrouse
25 cm
Along roadsides in daytime; flocks of up to 100 drink at waterholes in the evening; need a daily ration of water
Grouping: Pairs or family groups
Diet: Seeds & bulbs

A	E	I	M
B	F	J	N
C	G	K	O
D	H	L	P

Near rocky outcrops

886
Rock bunting
14 cm
Easily seen when perched prominently on rocky protrusion; nomadic when not breeding
Diet: Seeds; insects on the ground

593
Mocking chat
22 cm
(F) is not as colourful as (M); mimic a wide range of bird calls
Grouping: Pairs or small groups; 4-5 birds
Diet: Insects; fruit

(M)

A	E	I	M
B	F	J	N
C	G	K	O
D	H	L	P

Birds in dry bushveld (continued)

In open bush or on ground nearby

764 Glossy starling
23 cm
Usually feed off the ground; also forage in trees
Grouping: Pairs breeding; non-breeding flocks 6-10
Diet: Omnivorous, mainly insects and fruit

762 Burchell's starling
32 cm
Large starling; black eye; very noisy
Grouping: Solitary or pairs; small groups
Diet: Mainly insects; also fruit

765 Greater blue-eared starling
22 cm
Most common starling in the KNP
Habitat: Particularly common in camp & picnic sites; roost communally
Grouping: Breeding pairs; non-breedin gregarious in large flocks
Diet: Omnivorous, mainly fruit

459 Yellowbilled hornbill
48-60 cm
Habitat: Often seen in camp sites & picnic spots; forage on ground & in trees; can be tame
Grouping: Solitary or pairs; small groups
Breeding: In breeding season (Oct – Nov), pairs bob up & down while calling together
Diet: Rodents; insects; scorpions; seeds; fruit

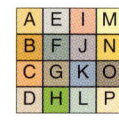

458 Redbilled hornbill
46 cm
Forage on ground; dig for food in soil & dung
Habitat: Overgrazed areas; Mopane woodland
Grouping: Pairs; non-breeding, gregarious, small flocks
Breeding: Like all hornbills (F) is sealed off in nest, where she loses all her feathers, during laying and incubation; during this time, she is fed by (M) through small opening
Diet: Insects; seeds; scorpions; amphibians

580 Groundscraper thrush
21 cm
Most often seen on lawns of restcamps; search under leaves and debris for food – hence the name
Grouping: Solitary or pairs; sometimes groups
Diet: Insects & variety of worms; berries

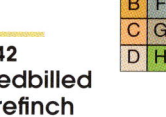

842 Redbilled firefinch
10 cm
(F) more brown than (M); often seen with other seed-eaters
Habitat: Acacia thornveld with open patches near watercourses
Grouping: Pairs or small parties
Diet: Seeds

(M)

451 Hoopoe
27 cm
Conspicuous crest can be erected into fan; call from perch in tree
Grouping: Solitary or pairs; non-breeding small groups
Diet: Insects; earthworms; small snakes; frogs

846 Common waxbill
13 cm
Habitat: Taller, thicker grass; along rivers & dams
Grouping: Breeding pairs or family groups; non-breeding gregarious flocks, up to 30 birds
Diet: Grass seeds, often taken green from seed-heads

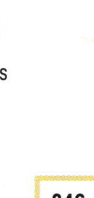

On flowering plants

844 Blue waxbill
13 cm
Most common waxbill
Grouping: Breeding pairs; non-breeding gregarious, up to 40 birds
Breeding: Often build nest close to wasp nest for protection
Diet: Seeds on ground

793 Collared sunbird
11 cm
Shorter bill than most sunbirds; feed in low bush
Grouping: Usually pairs; family groups; aggressive, territorial (M)
Diet: Mainly insects

791 Scarletchested sunbird
14 cm
(F) very drab compared with (M); more common in rest camps, where flowers grow, than in the veld
Grouping: Solitary or pairs, except at food source
Breeding: Nest consists of plant material woven together with spider webs
Diet: Mainly nectar

(M)

884 Goldenbreasted bunting
16 cm
Very common; show white outer-tail feathers when flushed; call from perch sounds like *"pretty boy-pretty boy-pretty boy"*
Grouping: Solitary or pairs; gregarious flocks, up to 20 birds
Diet: Mainly seeds; also insects

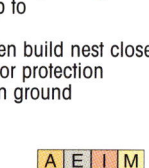

869 Yelloweyed canary
12 cm
Often in groups with other birds; often feeding on the ground; call likened to *"yes I see you"*
Grouping: Gregarious flocks 20-30
Diet: Seeds; insects on the ground

701
Chinspot batis
13 cm
Name derived
from rusty
chinspot in (F);
call likened to
"three blind mice" tune
Grouping: Solitary or pairs;
often in bird parties in summer
Breeding: (M) feeds (F) during courtship,
nest-building, egg laying & incubation
(Aug – Feb)
Diet: Insects; spiders

743
Threestreaked
tchagra
19 cm
Forage low down in
thickets & on the ground
Habitat: Woodland;
thornveld thickets
Diet: Insects

753
White helmetshrike
20 cm
Very restless birds, tend to move
continuously; each group has a territory
which is defended against other groups,
& it has only one breeding pair
Grouping: Gregarious; groups 5-22
Diet: Insects; spiders; rarely lizards

613
Whitebrowed
robin
15 cm
Territorial; secretive, hide deep in thick bush
& long grass; often sing for long periods
Grouping: Solitary
Diet: Insects; spiders; some berries; nectar

473
Crested
barbet
23 cm
Quite inconspicuous, unless foraging
on ground or calling; characteristic
trill can be heard all year, especially
in summer
Grouping: Solitary or pairs; small groups
Diet: Mainly insects; less fruit than
other barbets

560
Arrowmarked
babbler
24 cm
Raucous chorus of birds often
heard, but they are difficult
to see
Habitat: Forage on ground;
clamber through lower branches
Grouping: Gregarious; groups
of up to 10
Diet: Mainly insects & small
lizards

355
Laughing dove
25 cm
Does not have black ring around
neck; very common in KNP; must
drink water daily – often seen in big
groups at water points
Grouping: Solitary or pairs;
groups at water
Diet: Small seeds of herbs & grass; termites; small insects

358
Greenspotted
dove
20 cm
Often found feeding next to the road;
call is a distinctive bushveld sound,
ending in a mournful, descending
"tu-tu-tu-tu-tu-tu-tu"
Diet: Seeds; berries; termites

Birds active at night

Nocturnal

You can see these birds at dawn and dusk, or in the camps at night

401
Spotted eagle owl
45 cm
Superb hearing; tufts on head
are not ears; like other owls they
can move heads 180° to see
directly behind them
Habitat: Roost by day on rocky
ledge or in tree; pairs often sit
close together; presence is
often given away by chattering
of small birds
Diet: Large insects,
like grasshoppers;
small mammals;
birds

298
Water dikkop
40 cm
Habitat: Seldom
far from water
Grouping:
Solitary; pairs or
non-breeding flocks, 20-30 birds
Breeding: No nest, but lay eggs
on ground among driftwood
Diet: Insects; crustaceans; molluscs

405
Fierynecked nightjar
24 cm
Call *"Good Lord, deliver us"*,
especially at dusk and dawn; hawk
from a perch; very wide gaping mouths
Diet: Insects, especially beetles; spiders

Birds near permanent water

In large trees

A	E	I	M
B	F	J	N
C	G	K	O
D	**H**	L	P

148
African fish eagle
70 cm
Loud distinctive call
Habitat: Spend most of the day perched in large riverine trees
Grouping: Pairs; mate for life
Diet: Fish; sometimes birds

(F)

(M)

A	E	I	M
B	F	J	N
C	G	K	O
D	**H**	L	P

815
Lesser masked weaver
15 cm
Grouping: Gregarious; non-breeding (M) resembles (F)
Breeding: Aug – Feb; large breeding colonies, often in association with Spottedbacked weavers; nests small & neat in trees overhanging water
Diet: Insects; seeds; nectar

In reeds

A	E	I	M
B	F	J	N
C	G	K	O
D	**H**	L	P

371
Purplecrested lourie
42 cm
Very conspicuous red on wings when flying; call is loud "*kok - kok*" repeated many times
Grouping: Pairs; small groups
Breeding: Aug – Nov
Diet: Mainly fruit

361
Green pigeon
30 cm
Resemble parrots when clambering through trees
Habitat: Secretive, feed high in evergreen trees
Grouping: Gregarious
Diet: Fruit, especially figs

A	E	I	M
B	F	J	N
C	G	K	O
D	**H**	L	P

A	E	I	M
B	F	J	N
C	G	K	O
D	**H**	L	P

431
Malachite kingfisher
14 cm
Dive for prey from reeds & branches, overhanging quiet pools
Grouping: Solitary
Breeding: Build nests in sandy cliffs by excavating long tunnels with chambers
Diet: Fish; insects; tadpoles; frogs; crustaceans

On a prominent perch

(F)

(M)

(F)

(M)

A	E	I	M
B	F	J	N
C	G	K	O
D	**H**	L	P

429
Giant kingfisher
46 cm
Largest of the kingfishers; distinctive brown chest; hunt from perch above water
Grouping: Solitary; rarely pairs
Diet: Fish; crabs; frogs

428
Pied kingfisher
28 cm
Hover above water searching for fish; stun prey before eating
Grouping: Solitary or pairs; loose groups
Diet: Mainly fish

A	E	I	M
B	F	J	N
C	G	K	O
D	**H**	L	P

A	E	I	M
B	F	J	N
C	G	K	O
D	**H**	L	P

443
Whitefronted bee-eater
24 cm
Distinctive white & red throat; catch insects in the air; large groups seen in sandy river banks where they breed
Grouping: Solitary or small groups
Diet: Flying insects, especially butterflies

Near the water's edge

A	E	I	M
B	F	J	N
C	G	K	O
D	**H**	L	P

711
African pied wagtail
20 cm
Characteristic wagging of tail while searching for food
Habitat: Common on waterways & riverside camps
Grouping: Breeding pairs or groups
Diet: Small invertebrates; insects

A	E	I	M
B	F	J	N
C	G	K	O
D	**H**	L	P

258
Blacksmith plover
30 cm
Name refers to call that resembles metallic ring of hammer hitting an anvil
Grouping: Pairs; non-breeding, loose flocks, up to 30
Breeding: Like other plovers, chicks leave the nest almost immediately after hatching
Diet: Insects; worms; molluscs

A	E	I	M
B	F	J	N
C	G	K	O
D	**H**	L	P

94
Hadeda ibis
76 cm
The only vocal ibis; loud, clamorous "*ha-ha-de-da*"
Grouping: Gregarious; large non-breeding flocks, 5-20 birds
Diet: Mainly insects; they can also retrieve food from deep under the soil with their long bills

249
Threebanded plover
18 cm
Hunt by running short distances, then stopping to peck at prey
Grouping: Pairs; non-breeding flocks, up to 40
Breeding: Protect eggs & chicks by pretending to be injured & luring away predators
Diet: Mainly insects & spiders

A	E	I	M
B	F	J	N
C	G	K	O
D	**H**	L	P

64
Goliath heron
1,4 m
Largest heron in the world; hunt by standing stock-still in water waiting for prey; often seen standing knee-deep in water; call is a hoarse "*kraak*"
Grouping: Solitary
Diet: Mostly fish of 500-600 g

A E I M
B F J N
C G K O
D H L P

62
Grey heron
1 m
Commonly seen wading through shallow water, stalking prey
Grouping: Solitary
Diet: Mostly fish of 10-20 g

A E I M
B F J N
C G K O
D H L P

(M)
(F)

88
Saddlebilled stork
1,4 m
One of the endangered birds (less than 20 pairs in the KNP); every bird has a unique bill colour/pattern; notice the difference in eye colour & wattles (skin flaps) between (M) & (F)
Diet: Mainly fish

A E I M
B F J N
C G K O
D H L P

66
Great white egret
95 cm
(Breeding plumage illustrated)
Stand motionless for hours in shallow water watching for prey
Grouping: Solitary
Breeding: Bills change from yellow to black just before breeding season
Diet: Fish; frogs; insects; small mammals

95
African spoonbill
90 cm
Feed by moving partially-opened bill from side to side through water, to sieve out small food items
Grouping: Solitary or gregarious
Diet: Small fish; aquatic invertebrates

A E I M
B F J N
C G K O
D H L P

99
Whitefaced duck
48 cm
Very erect posture shows white face clearly; more often seen once rains have filled seasonal pans
Grouping: Gregarious flocks of up to ± 30
Diet: Underwater seeds & tubers of aquatic plants

A E I M
B F J N
C G K O
D H L P

A E I M
B F J N
C G K O
D H L P

60
Darter
79 cm
Swim with only head emerged, with long neck folded under water ready to spear prey; often seen sitting on perch drying wings
Grouping: Usually solitary
Diet: Fish; frogs; arthropods

A E I M
B F J N
C G K O
D H L P

A E I M
B F J N
C G K O
D H L P

55
Whitebreasted cormorant
90 cm
Not very common in the KNP, but unique as is the only cormorant with both riverine & marine populations
Grouping: Solitary or gregarious
Diet: Mainly fish

115
Knobbilled duck
(M) 80 cm,
(F) 65 cm
Only (M) has a knob; often seen at temporary pools after rain
Grouping: Breeding pairs or small groups
Breeding: Polygamous, 1 (M): 3 (F)
Diet: Seeds & tubers of water plants

(M)

A E I M
B F J N
C G K O
D H L P

81
Hamerkop
56 cm
Feed in shallow water (or even flood water); tread & stir mud to flush prey
Grouping: Solitary or pairs; small groups
Breeding: Huge, untidy nest, made by 1-4 birds & used for generations; superstition suggests it is unlucky to disturb a nest
Diet: Mostly tadpoles & frogs; also fish

A E I M
B F J N
C G K O
D H L P

102
Egyptian goose
70 cm
Very common; call often heard: (F) honks "*honk honk haaaa*", (M) hisses
Grouping: Pairs; non-breeding gregarious
Breeding: Use disused raptor or Hamerkop nests; also nest on rocky ledges
Diet: Grass; sedges; herbs

A E I M
B F J N
C G K O
D H L P

240
African jacana
28 cm
Walk on lily pads on extraordinary long feet
Grouping: Solitary or pairs; small loose groups
Breeding: (F) has many mates in one season; (M) takes care of chicks, sometimes carrying them under wings
Diet: Mainly aquatic insects

Michael Thayer

79

Reptiles, insects and other small creatures

The Kruger National Park is home to dozens of reptiles and thousands of species of insects. The descriptions and pictures below will help you to find some of the more obvious ones. Take note of where they occur and at what time of day to look for them. If you keep your eyes open, you will find many fascinating creatures.

To help you judge the size of the creatures, they are recorded as follows:
Length: In millimetres, centimetres or metres
Weight: In kilograms
(M) = Male; (F) = Female

Further reading:
Field Guide to Insects of the Kruger National Park
– Leo Braack
Field Guide to the Snakes and other Reptiles of Southern Africa
– Bill Branch

Reptiles

Reptiles are cold-blooded and need to absorb energy from the sun. During the winter months they are easy to spot, warming themselves on exposed rocks, tree trunks or sand banks.

Throughout the Park

Nile crocodile
Crocodylus niloticus
2,5-3,5 m; 70-100 kg
(may exceed 1000 kg)
Grouping: Communal
Breeding: 16-80 eggs are laid in nest-site in sunny bank; defended by (F); after they hatch young carried to the water in her mouth; attentive parents
Diet: Fish; antelope; carrion

Flap-neck chamaeleon
Chamaeleo dilepis
20-24 cm
Habitat: Savannah woodland
Grouping: Only pair up for mating
Breeding: (F) digs tunnel & lays 25-50 eggs (may take up to 24 hours); hatch in 150-300 days, depending on temperature
Diet: Insects, especially grasshoppers & beetles

Blue-headed tree agama
Stelio atricollis
20-30 cm
Habitat: Open savannah, particularly with Acacias
Breeding: (F) lays 8-14 oval, soft-shelled eggs in a hole dug in moist soil; hatch after 90 days
Diet: Termites; insects

Rainbow rock skink
Mabuya quinquetaeniata
18-24 cm; max 29 cm
Juveniles & adult females have electric blue tails
Habitat: Dry savannah
Breeding: Summer; (F) lays 6-10 eggs
Diet: Mainly insects

African rock python
Python sebae natalensis
3-5 m; max 5,6 m
Habitat: Woodland, often near permanent water
Breeding: Lay 30-50 eggs in disused burrows; protected by (F); hatch in 65-80 days
Diet: Small antelope; monkeys; fish; ground roosting birds; rodents; (kill by constricting prey)

Always near water

Leguaan (Rock monitor)
Varanus exanthematicus
More heavily built than the Nile/Water monitor; thicker head; blunter nose
0,7-1,0 m; max 1,3 m
Habitat: Dry savannah; trunks, holes & disused animal burrows
Grouping: Usually solitary; hibernates
Breeding: Aug – Sep; (F) may lay 8-37 eggs in active termite nest; otherwise in hole in moist soil; take 1 year to hatch
Diet: Millipedes; beetles; grasshoppers; carrion; baby tortoises

Leguaan (Nile/Water monitor)
Varanus niloticus
1,0-1,4 m; max 2,1 m
Largest African lizard; excellent swimmer
Habitat: In vegetation alongside larger rivers & dams
Breeding: Aug – Sep, after first rains; (F) lays 20-60 eggs in active termite nest; incubated at constant temperature & humidity; may take 1 year to hatch
Diet: Crabs; mussels; fish; frogs; birds; eggs; insects

Mike Parkin

Insects

Insects are the biggest group of all creatures in the KNP. They are essential to the maintenance of the balance in the ecosystem. They return food material directly into the soil and they play a vital role in pollinating plants. They are on average the most colourful of all the KNP's wildlife! Look out for them around the camp fires at night, and in trees during the day.

Always near water

Dragonfly
Odonata

Different varieties with wingspans 4,5-14 cm
Habitat: Large rivers & dams
Breeding: (F) lays eggs while skimming the water; eggs drift to the bottom & young (nymphs) hatch after a few days; nymphs propel themselves forward by sucking in water & squirting it out
Diet: Adults & nymphs feed on insects

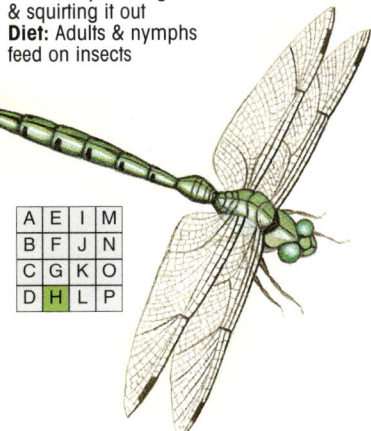

A	E	I	M
B	F	J	N
C	G	K	O
D	H	L	P

Koppie charaxes
Charaxes jasius saturnus

Over 200 species of butterfly are seen regularly; charaxes are particularly spectacular, with tail-like extensions on their hind-wings
Diet: Can often be seen sucking fluid from elephant dung or the sap of damaged trees

A	E	I	M
B	F	J	N
C	G	K	O
D	H	L	P

Honeybee
Apis mellifera adansonii

Very important insects as they make honey and pollinate plants
Habitat: Widespread with hives often in rock crevices
Grouping: Well-ordered social communities
Breeding: Each hive has one queen, which mates with (M) bees (drones), and lays thousands of eggs a day in summer
Diet: Nectar; pollen

A	E	I	M
B	F	J	N
C	G	K	O
D	H	L	P

Mopane emperor moth & worm
Gonimbrasia belina

Have large "eye" spots on wings; adult moths are nocturnal
Habitat: Caterpillars are found only in summer in Mopane trees
Utilization: A delicacy for birds & man

A	E	I	M
B	F	J	N
C	G	K	O
D	H	L	P

Throughout the Park

Cicada (Christmas beetle)
Cicadidae

20 mm
Found throughout KNP; seldom seen, because of their perfect camouflage; singing in summer is a characteristic sound of Lowveld bush; sound made by leg muscles vibrating against a special membrane
Breeding: Adults live for only a few weeks – to find a mate, copulate & lay eggs; nymphs that hatch from the eggs live underground for many years before emerging

A	E	I	M
B	F	J	N
C	G	K	O
D	H	L	P

Locust
Orthoptera

Many are cryptically coloured to hide them in vegetation
Habitat: Wide variety
Grouping: Red locust can form huge swarms on northern plains
Breeding: Eggs are normally laid in a hole in the soil
Diet: Vegetation
Utilization: Important source of food for mammals, birds & lizards

A	E	I	M
B	F	J	N
C	G	K	O
D	H	L	P

Termite (white ant/flying ant)
Macrotermes michaelsenii

Habitat: Live in huge termitaria (anthills); structure of the termitaria regulates both temperature & humidity conditions perfectly
Utilization: Important food source for aardvark & birds

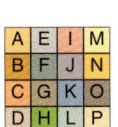

A	E	I	M
B	F	J	N
C	G	K	O
D	H	L	P

A	E	I	M
B	F	J	N
C	G	K	O
D	H	L	P

Anopheles mosquito
Anophelinae

Only (F) carries malaria; common throughout the KNP from Oct – May
Habitat: Abundant mainly along rivers, streams, pans & waterholes; malaria mosquitoes breed in shallow rain pools & therefore occur everywhere
Breeding: Lay eggs in standing water
Diet: (M) feeds on juice of rotting fruit; (F) sucks blood; feed (bite) actively, from dusk to dawn

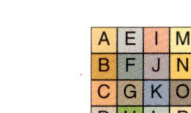

A	E	I	M
B	F	J	N
C	G	K	O
D	H	L	P

Dung beetle
Scarabaeinae

50 mm
Clean up decaying matter & carry the nutrients underground
Habitat: Very common in the KNP; many species of different sizes
Breeding: Often seen rolling balls of dung in which they lay one egg; balls are buried to maintain moisture & provide protection against predators

Antlion
Myrmeleonidae

12 mm
Adults resemble dragonflies; mostly nocturnal
Habitat: Conical pits in sandy areas, often seen at picnic sites
Diet: Larvae prey on ants & other crawling insects which slip down & are trapped in the sandy pit

A	E	I	M
B	F	J	N
C	G	K	O
D	H	L	P

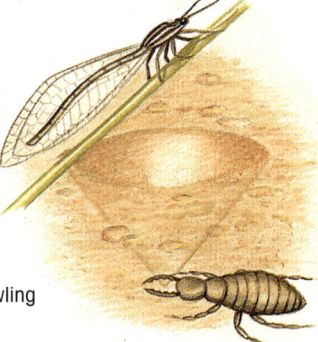

Other small creatures

Throughout the Park

Community spider
Stegodyphus dumicola
Very small
Grouping: Live socially
Breeding: For protection they make large bird-like nests, with many spiders in one nest
Diet: Threads spun around the nest catch prey, which is shared by all occupants of nest
Utilization: Web used by some birds in their nest building

Golden orbweb spider
Nephila senegalensis
25-30 mm
Large spider; spectacular, golden, orb-shaped webs, seen early in the morning laden with dew
Diet: Insects, captured in web

Transvaal thick-tailed scorpion
Parabuthus transvaalicus
Up to 14 cm
Related to spiders; stings can be dangerous to humans; thick tail, small pinchers
Habitat: Under stones; in burrows & dead logs
Diet: Insects; spiders; small lizards; other scorpions

Millipede (Songololo)
Diplopoda
Up to 20 cm
Some varieties defend themselves with poisonous fluid (containing hydrogen cyanide) from headglands; roll into a ball when disturbed
Habitat: Usually found in moist places
Diet: Plant-eating, preferring rotten leaves

Giant land snail
Achatina
13-20 cm
Can be seen in the early morning after rain; usually nocturnal; can live up to 10 years
Breeding: Lay up to 500 eggs annually
Diet: Omnivorous, eating dead animals & plants

Leopard tortoise
Geochelone pardalis babcocki
30-45 cm, max 72 cm; 8-12 kg
Breeding: Mating (at 15 years old) is fairly robust, with the (M) pushing & butting the (F) into submission; 6-15 eggs are laid in a hole in the ground
Diet: Wide variety of plants; fruit

Olive toad
Bufo garmani
3-5 cm
Habitat: On land in damp places
Diet: Insects, especially termites & moths; nocturnal hunters

Serrated hinged terrapin
Pelusios sinuatus
30-40 cm
Habitat: Often seen basking on rocks & logs during the day
Diet: Carrion; mussels; invertebrates; frogs; even take ticks off the legs of buffalo drinking water

Always near water

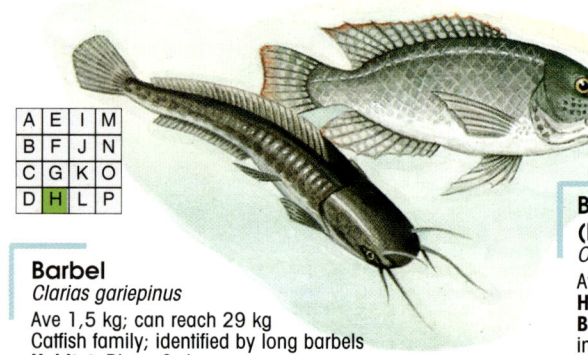

Barbel
Clarias gariepinus
Ave 1,5 kg; can reach 29 kg
Catfish family; identified by long barbels
Habitat: Rivers & dams
Diet: Omnivorous scavenger, foraging mostly at night
Utilization: Important in the diet of crocodiles

Blue kurper (Mozambique tilapia)
Oreochromis mossambicus
Ave 1 kg
Habitat: Slow-flowing rivers
Breeding: (M) scoops a depression in sandbed of pool for (F) to lay eggs; these are sucked into her mouth where they are kept until hatching
Diet: Omnivorous

Foam nest frog
Chiromantis xerampelina
7-8 cm
Habitat: Tree branches overhanging water
Breeding: Eggs mixed into a foam nest; tadpoles hatch here & drop into water
Diet: Tadpoles feed on algae & decaying vegetation

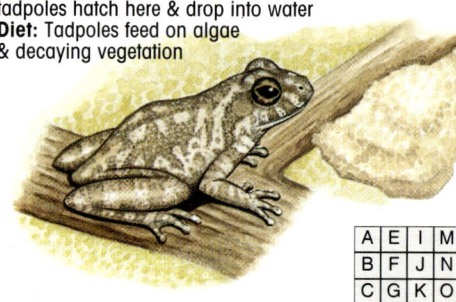

EVERYTHING IN NATURE IS LINKED

The first part of this book shows how geology, plants and animals depend on one another for healthy survival in the Kruger National Park.
The following pages outline the history of humans in the Lowveld, from the earliest inhabitants to the establishment of Kruger as a National Park.

Over the past 100 years the Earth has supported humans to achieve the technological heights that make our lives safer and more comfortable.

The environment throughout the planet has paid a heavy price for man's development.

It is important to remember that wherever we live, whatever our life style and environment... everything around us is linked back to Earth.

This link must be maintained at all costs. As you travel home, remember how important every link in the chain is... and at home, you too can play an important role to keep these links healthy and viable.

HISTORY

Over thousands of years people have lived in what is today the Kruger National Park. They did not change the environment very much and so today we can imagine what life must have been like here for human beings in the distant past. At first it must have been a short and brutish existence, but as time went by, humans began to conquer nature, and survival in this wild place became easier. Our relationship with nature has developed from one of co-existence to one of destruction and abuse, and finally to conservation. Today we face the challenges of the present to determine the future, but we do this with the knowledge of the past ...

32

The numbers in this section correspond with the numbered icons on the *Maps* (pages 24-35), as well as with those summarised on the small history map on page 87.

The numbers on the *Maps* follow numerical sequence (1-75), from the north to the south.

I STONE AGE

Stones and bones

Archaeologists have discovered that early humans roamed through the Lowveld as far back as one and a half million years ago. These ancient humans *(Homo erectus)* left clues for us about their prehistoric lives, such as stone tools, their skeletons and the bones of the animals they ate. From this evidence we can get some idea of how they lived and what they looked like.

The average brain size of *Homo erectus* was 935 cubic centimetres, compared with modern people's 1 345 cubic centimetres. Heaps of bones that have been found of now extinct animals, like the mammoth, the short-necked giraffe and the oversized baboon, show they hunted, but they mainly scavenged and foraged for food. Stone tools from this time have been found at the confluences of the Luvuvhu and Limpopo, as well as the Letaba and Olifants Rivers. This is proof that they were 'human', because their actions were planned and their artifacts were designed for specific purposes. But early humans had to adapt to, and move with, a changing climate. Sometimes dwelling sites were evacuated for thousands of years as the people moved off to find better game and a favourable climate.

During the Middle Stone Age (100 000-40 000 BC) humans gradually became more refined. Today we find ourselves in the 'space age', but the human capacity for invention began a long, long time ago.

San hunter-gatherer

The San – inventors and artists

The Late Stone Age began 40 000 years ago. "Necessity is the mother of invention", and in order to survive, *Homo sapiens* learnt to develop more efficient tools and weapons. Small bands of nomadic hunter-gatherers, known as the San, lived and moved through the Lowveld. There were giant leaps in technology with advances like fishing hooks, tools for gathering food, and the bow and arrow (developed about 10 000 years ago). Poisoned arrows made hunting easier. They were made from the poison bush, certain *Euphorbia* trees, poison rope, and the venom of snakes and spiders. These developments gave the San time to refine their tools and weapons even more – and it gave them time to paint.

On a rock face at Renosterkoppies, there is a painting that dates back thousands of years. It is one of about 150 San engraving and painting sites found so far in Kruger. These paintings were central to the San's rituals and religion and give us a glimpse of their spiritual beliefs and practices, and their dances and trances which healed the sick and connected them with the spirit world. The paintings also depict nature which for them was both earthly and divine. It is thought that the San used egg white, animal fat and blood as binding agents for coloured pigments. Hair from the manes and tails of animals was carefully made into the first paint brushes. They also used feathers and their fingers to record glimpses of life in the Stone Age.
(site 56 on the Wolhuter Trail, and site 63).

II IRON AGE

The first farmers

For centuries the San lived without competition for resources. But as early as 200 AD, more technologically advanced people, the Bantu-speaking farmers, immigrated into the Lowveld and settled along the banks of the Limpopo, Luvuvhu, Shingwedzi, Letaba and later the Sabie and Crocodile Rivers. They brought crops and herds of domestic animals and the secret of metal-work. This was the beginning of the Iron Age in southern Africa.

Archaeologists have discovered that for hundreds of years this new civilisation lived alongside the San, sharing the abundance provided by the bush. As more people moved into the area, the San were gradually pushed out, although scattered groups still inhabited the area as late as the 19th century.

The new farmers were still dependant on their environment. There is evidence that, between 800-1600 AD, the area suffered poor farming conditions, game became scarcer, and many groups moved off to better pastures. Those who stayed relied on hunting and trade.

Fingerprinting the past

In Kruger archaeologists have identified different periods by the different types of pottery that were made. So far more than 12 different cultural groups have been identified, some dating back to 200 AD. Each form of pottery is like a fingerprint of a different time and group of people. Beautiful 'fluted' clay vessels have been found near Mopane Camp and at Silver Leaves, close to Tzaneen. This is the earliest archaeological record of the early farmers in South Africa. These vessels show the fine craftsmanship of the first black settler farmers as far back as the second century AD.

Tsonga woman

Early trade – black, white and yellow gold

International trade in South Africa began about 1 000 years before gold was discovered on the Witwatersrand. Copper from Phalaborwa and Balule (site 21), salt from Eiland, and crops like sorghum and beans, had long been traded locally. But the Lowveld and the interior had far more exotic goods that attracted the attention of Arab traders in search of riches and new products. Africa had 'white gold', in the form of elephant ivory. It had yellow gold, the precious metal that kings and sultans desired. And in the Late Iron Age, it had 'black gold' – the slaves.

The interest from Arab traders in the 9th and 10th centuries, resulted in the rise of the Mapungubwe kingdom, based at the confluence of the Limpopo and Shashe Rivers (current Zimbabwe / Botswana border). Trade goods were brought from Arab seaports on the east coast, like Sofala. This affected people living in and around today's Kruger National Park, who soon formed states allied to Mapungubwe, at places like Makahane and Shilowa (1000-1300 AD).

After 1200 AD Great Zimbabwe succeeded Mapungubwe as the inland trade capital. In the Lowveld, stone-built royal dwellings were constructed

Masorini Stone Age Site

at Thulamela, Matekevhele and other sites (visit Thulamela by appointment – site 11). Dzundzwini, (site 9) meaning 'the fields that belong to the chief and the people' provided food to traders and visitors to the royal enclosure. Another interesting historical name from this period is Gumbandebuu, which means 'the shearing of the beards' and refers to the Venda initiation school that led young men symbolically and religiously into adulthood.

These chiefdoms left testimony to a profitable international trade – glass beads, Chinese porcelain, home-woven and imported cloth, ivory bracelets, gold, bronze, copper and iron artifacts and jewellery. Much of the iron produced was traded with the agriculturally rich areas of the eastern escarpment. Masorini, once also a Stone Age site, was still a powerful centre for the production of iron tools and weapons in the 19th century.

Standing at this prehistoric site (site 19), one is struck by the power of images from thousands of years ago. In the words of Prof. Hannes Eloff, *"it is as if the actors have left the stage, but the set remains intact"*.

III EUROPEAN EXPLORERS

White man's grave

It wasn't until 1725 that the first European encountered the hostile Lowveld. Francois de Cuiper, a Dutchman, crossed the Lebombo Mountains. No sooner had he entered the present day Kruger National Park, than he was attacked at Gomondwane (site 61) and beat a hasty retreat to the coast. For another century the area remained a mystery to adventurous Europeans, who had already circumnavigated the world but had not yet conquered or colonised Africa or its people. In time the Lowveld became known as 'the white man's grave'.

The first European to return was João Albasini, a Portuguese trader who ventured from Delagoa Bay (Maputo) in 1830, and began establishing tradelinks inland. Albasini's larger than life personality, his willingness to learn local language, and the help of the warrior chiefs Manungu and Jozikhulu, enabled him to survive. People living along the Sabie River felt they were under his protection and in turn protected him (sites 33, 51, 58).

By this time, the Voortrekker people had settled in the Transvaal. It became imperative, if they were to escape the fetters of the British Empire, that they

Albasini ruins

discover the ancient African trade routes to the east coast. Lang Hans van Rensberg and his small group left Zoutpansberg in 1836 . They were never seen again. His compatriot, Louis Trichardt, set out to find him and to open the route to Delagoa Bay. João Albasini was there to meet the survivors of the gruelling trek. Trichardt, his wife and most of his people, died of malaria. (sites relating to this period are 6, 15, 26, 50, 57, 60; other trade sites are 64, 65, 67, 69, 73).

Golden years – prospectors, crooks and hunters

In 1873, gold was discovered in the Lowveld. Hordes of fortune-seeking prospectors flooded in. More than ever, it was necessary to establish links with the east coast in order to get food and machinery for the miners. (sites 12, 48). A Hungarian man, Alois Nellmapius, was contracted to build the road to Delagoa Bay. Sir Percy FitzPatrick used this route for his transport riders. Memorials to FitzPatrick's famous Staffordshire terrier, Jock, can be seen at sites 49, 68, 71.

At the same time, the Lowveld attracted many criminals and hunters (sites 13, 74). Colourful characters, like Bvekenya Barnard of Ivory Trail fame, made their living from selling ivory, both legally and illegally. Those escaping the law headed for "Crooks' Corner" (site 3), which borders on three countries – South Africa, Moçambique and Zimbabwe. From here they only needed to hop across one of three borders to safety. (other sites are 1, 8)

Jock of the Bushveld memorial

'A mad and delightful mania'

The free and romantic lifestyle attracted fearless and eccentric characters, like Barnard and William Cornwallis-Harris. The latter said of himself that he found hunting *"a truly most delightful mania."* As time went by, many hunters realised they could not survive off ivory trade alone. They turned from the white gold of ivory to the black gold of recruiting labour for the Witwatersrand mines.

Cheap labour, WNLA and the pass laws

"In the midst of trouble and sorrow we left our children at home, children full of tears, crying tears; ...

father is gone, is gone; God, help fathers to return." (From **Another Blanket**. Agency of Industrial Mission). These words were sung by prospective recruitments for the Witwatersrand gold mines at the turn of the century.

For some years, labour was illegally traded from the present day Kruger, but later only the Witwatersrand Native Labour Association was allowed to recruit (sites 4, 5). Once in Johannesburg, the labourers lived in appalling conditions, but migrant labour continued to be the mainstay of South Africa's mining industry.

IV THE BEGINNING OF KNP

The first reserve and forced removals

By the end of the century, hunting mania had wiped out the Lowveld's huge herds of game. In 1898, President Paul Kruger proclaimed the area between the Crocodile and Sabie Rivers as the Sabie Reserve. This was fortunate timing as for the next 4 years, politicians, hunters and fortune-seekers were too busy fighting the Anglo-Boer war to care about conservation (site 66).

After the war the British victors reproclaimed the Reserve (site 20 relates to this period). They set about clearing the way for the protected area. This involved the forced removal of local inhabitants and in 1903, between 2 000-3 000 people were moved out of the Sabie Reserve. Similar removals were conducted throughout Kruger's history. In 1969, after many years of dispute, the Makuleke people were moved out of the Pafuri area. Land claims today continue the dispute between the need to conserve a natural heritage, and the people's need for both land and work.

He who turns things upside down

Major James Stevenson-Hamilton was appointed the first warden and told to manage a piece of land the size of the Netherlands. The short statured, short tempered Scotsman achieved this and earned himself the name 'Skukuza', meaning he who turns things upside down. Stevenson waged war on poaching and managed to persuade the government to expand the Reserve to include the whole area between the Crocodile and Luvuvhu Rivers. Farmers voiced stiff opposition, accusing the Reserve of being "a breeding ground for lions". Both domestic stock and people were often attacked, as men like Harry Wolhuter could testify. Possibly South Africa's most famous ranger, he was attacked by lions in 1903. As the big male dragged him off, he felt for its heart and stabbed it fatally with his pocket knife (site 27).

Living in solitude, far from any form of civilisation, rangers like Wolhuter, Gaza Gray, Helfas Nkuna, Jafuta Shithlave, Njinja Ndlovu and G.R. Healy laid the foundations for the Kruger National Park. Today we still enjoy the benefits of their energy and vision (sites 29, 32, 34, 35, 37, 55).

A train reaction

A deciding factor in the creation of the Kruger National Park, was the Eastern and Selati railway lines (relevant sites are 44, 45, 47, 62). By the time the lines were completed in 1912, very little gold was being mined in the Selati gold fields. In order to make the railway profitable, a 9 day tour of the Lowveld and Moçambique

was started. The most popular part of the tour proved to be the game viewing and a night under the stars at present day Skukuza. The fact that people would pay to see game, not just to shoot it, gave Stevenson-Hamilton the support he needed to proclaim the Reserve a National Park.

Word, deed and law

If Paul Kruger had spoken the first word regarding the protection of the Lowveld's wildlife, and James Stevenson-Hamilton had been the first to physically protect it, then Piet Grobler, Minister of Lands in 1926, takes the credit for legalising the reserve as a National Park (site 22). He successfully passed the Bill on National Parks through the government and named the area Kruger National Park. Private landowners, like Eileen Orpen (sites 23, 30), with a love of wildlife, donated land to the Park, increasing its size. The protection of all wildlife within the Park, and the development of tourism, were now official policy and the road forward was clear.

In 1927 three cars entered the Park. Two years later there were 850 cars. And over the next 50 years some 150 000 people visited the Kruger National Park annually. Today there are 700 000 wildlife enthusiasts who visit every year, enjoying the fruits of a long, fascinating and hard-won battle to create one of the finest Game Parks in the world.
(The following sites refer to development of Kruger, but do not appear in the text 2, 7, 10, 14, 16-18, 24, 25, 28, 31, 36, 38-43, 46, 52-54, 59, 70, 72, 75).

 Further reading:
Neem uit die verlede – Dr U de V Pienaar
South African Eden – James Stevenson-Hamilton

Stevenson-Hamilton memorial

Historical sites

The colours used on this page tie up with the colours of the headings on pages 84-86. These historical sites are also marked in the same way on the **Maps** (pages 24-35).

- 🟧 **The Stone Age**
- 🟨 **The Iron Age**
- 🟩 **European Explorers**
- 🟦 **The Beginning of KNP**

1 Bobomeni Drift
2 Old Pafuri tented camp site (at picnic site)
* 3 "Crooks' Corner"
* 4 WNLA recruiting station
5 Baobab Hill
6 Potgieter's route
7 Donations acknowledged
8 Klopperfontein Drift
9 Dzundwini Spring (also Ranger J.J. Coetzer's quarters)
10 Early bore-hole
11 Thulamela Iron Age site
12 Red Rocks
13 Bowker Kop
14 Old Shawu picnic site (Mooi Plaas)
15 Das Neves' cross
16 Anna Ledeboer's grave – ranger's wife
17 Engelhard plaque (Dam)
18 Ranger L.H. Ledeboer's quarters
19 Masorini historical site
20 Von Wielligh's baobab
21 Balule (Reitz's pontoon)
22 Grobler plaque (Dam)
23 Orpen memorial (Orpen)
24 Original hut at Rabelais' entrance gate (small museum)
* 25 William Lloyd's grave
26 Trichardt's memorial
27 Ranger Harry Wolhuter's lion attack plaque
28 Sausage tree where ranger G.C.S. Crous erected his "wattle-and-daub" quarters (at Tshokwane)
29 Kruger memorial tablets
30 Orpen memorial koppie
31 Acknowledgement to rangers (Paul Kruger Gate)
32 Paul Kruger monument (Paul Kruger Gate)
33 Albasini Ruins/ information display
34 Wolhuter's camp "Doispane"
35 Wolhuter's outspan (Spanplek)
36 De Laporte's windmill
37 Stevenson-Hamilton memorial library & information centre
38 Board member W.A. Campbell hut/museum
39 Pet cemetery (Skukuza)
40 Struben cottage (Skukuza)
41 Papenfus' clock tower (Skukuza)
42 Memorial to honour the founders of KNP
43 Pontoon crossing
44 Selati line and rail bridge
45 Selati train restaurant and museum (Skukuza)
46 First bore-hole (Skukuza)
47 Huhla siding (Skukuza)
48 Prospectors' graves
49 Jock of the Bushveld's plaque
50 Pretorius' grave
* 51 Manungu's kraal
52 "Wattle-and-daub" hut, built for tourists 1930 (Pretoriuskop)
53 Wolhuter's windmill
54 Board member Joe Ludorf plaque (Napi Kop)
55 Stevenson-Hamilton memorial & "grave" (Shirimantanga Koppie)
56 Bushman paintings (Wolhuter Trail)
57 Old Delagoa – Lydenburg wagon road
58 Albasini's trading post (Lower Sabie)
59 Duke's windmill
60 Sardelli's store
61 Francois de Cuiper's attack
62 Crocodile River railway bridge
63 Bushman paintings (Crocodile Bridge hippo pool)
64 Old trade route
65 Alf Roberts' trading store
66 General Ben Viljoen's attack site
67 Outspan plaques
68 Jock of the Bushveld & Sable statue (Jock camp)
69 Outspan plaque
70 First concrete dam (Ntomeni Spruit)
71 Jock of the Bushveld's birth place
72 Early bore-hole (Komapiti)
73 Thomas Hart's grave
74 Stols Nek (on Wolhuter Trail)
75 Harold Trollope hut (Malelane)

*Sites not accessible to visitors at time of print

PAFURI
*Makahane
*Matekevhele
PUNDA MARIA
SHINGWEDZI
*Shilowa
MOPANI
PHALABORWA
LETABA
OLIFANTS
SATARA
ORPEN
PAUL KRUGER
SKUKUZA
LOWER SABIE
NUMBI
PRETORIUSKOP
• Renoster-koppies
BERG-EN-DAL
CROCODILE BRIDGE
MALELANE

NATIONAL PARKS BOARD
Your Green Heritage

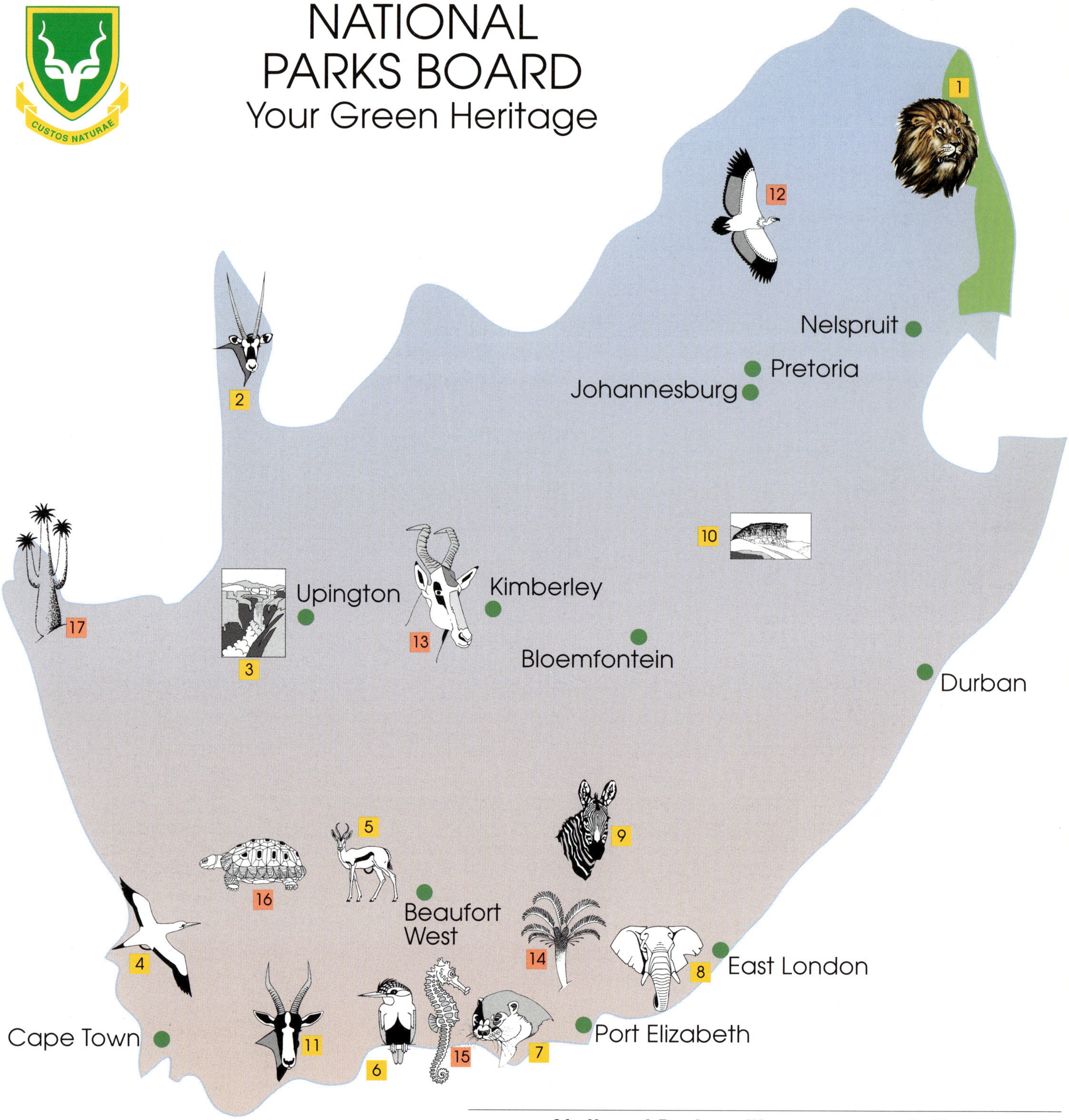

CUSTOS NATURAE

Nelspruit

Johannesburg • Pretoria

Upington

Kimberley

Bloemfontein

Durban

Beaufort West

East London

Cape Town

Port Elizabeth

National Parks with accommodation

1	Kruger National Park	7	Tsitsikamma National Park
2	Kalahari Gemsbok National Park	8	Addo Elephant National Park
3	Augrabies Falls National Park	9	Mountain Zebra National Park
4	West Coast National Park	10	Golden Gate Highlands National Park
5	Karoo National Park	11	Bontebok National Park
6	Wilderness National Park		

National Parks without accommodation

12	Kransberg National Park	15	Knysna National Lake Area
13	Vaalbos National Park	16	Tankwa Karoo National Park
14	Zuurberg National Park	17	Richtersveld National Park

For bookings phone: (012) 343-1991 • (021) 22-2810

88

GLOSSARY

Amphibian: a creature that lives partly on land and partly in water

Animals: all creatures in the animal kingdom i.e. mammals, birds, reptiles, insects and other small creatures

Annual: a plant that only grows for one growth season

Aquatic: an animal or plant that lives in water

Arthropod: an animal that has a jointed body, covered in a fairly hard, outer shell e.g. spider, scorpion, millipede, insect etc.

Browser: an animal that mainly eats leaves

Camouflage: the way that an animal's skin colour and texture blends with the surroundings, to hide it from predators

Carnivore: an animal that eats meat (carnivorous)

Carrion: meat of a dead animal (sometimes rotten)

Compound leaf: a single leaf that consists of many leaflets

Crown: the shape made by the upper branches and leaves of the tree

Crustacean: an animal with hard outer shell and many legs e.g. crab

Deciduous: a plant that loses its leaves during the winter

Disturbed area: an area that has been dug up, altered by man, or heavily grazed

Diurnal: an animal that is active during the day

Ecozone: an area with similar geology, rainfall and land-shape and therefore its own unique combination of plants and animals

Eco-habitat: an area of uniform vegetation and land-shape within an Ecozone

Ecosystem: an area where a number of different elements occur together naturally and depend on one another for healthy survival

Escarpment: the eastern Transvaal escarpment is the steep break between the Highveld and the Lowveld

Evergreen: a plant that does not lose its leaves in winter

Forb: a self-stemmed annual that dies back each winter and sprouts from seed after rain

Gondwanaland: one of the original super continents made up of Africa, Antarctica, Australia, India, Madagascar and South America

Grazer: an animal that mainly eats grass and roots

Gregarious: an animal that generally chooses to live in groups

Herbivore: an animal that eats plants (herbivorous)

Insectivore: an animal that eats insects (insectivorous)

Intrusion: (geology) new rock formation that is forced through an existing rock face while still in a liquid form

Invertibrates: an animal that does not have a boney spine

Larva: insect, from time of leaving egg, until changing into pupa

Latex: the milky liquid in the stems and leaves of certain plants

Mammal: an animal that gives birth to live young that feed on the mother's milk

Matriarch: a female that is the leader of her herd/pride/flock

Migrant: a bird that does not spend all year in one place; it moves to warmer areas when it gets cold as food is scarce

Mollusc: a soft-bodied animal covered by outer shell e.g. snail

Nocturnal: an animal that is active during the night

Omnivore: an animal that eats meat and plants (omnivorous)

Palatability: how tasty an animal finds a plant

Perennial: a plant that does not die back each year, and continues to increase in size until it reaches maturity

Pod: hard outer shell that protects fruit/seeds

Polygamous: a male animal that has more than one mate at a time

Predator: an animal (carnivore) that hunts and kills other creatures for food

Prey: an animal that is hunted and eaten as food

Primate: a specific type of mammal e.g. monkey and baboon

Pupa: insect in inactive, pre-adult form (cocoon)

Raptor: a bird that kills animals for food

Savannah: veld that is mainly grassland with scattered trees and/or shrubs (closed savannah has a greater number of trees and shrubs on it than open savannah)

Scavenger: an animal that does not hunt and kill all its own meat, but eats meat killed by other hunters (predators)

Sedge: a grass-like plant growing in marshes

Seepline: the line on a slope where soil and clay meet, and where water can come out onto the surface

Solitary: an animal that generally chooses to live alone

Sour grass: grass that is not palatable (tasty) and usually only eaten by grazers when it is young and tender

Sweet grass: grass that is palatable (tasty) and chosen by grazers as food when it is available

Termitarium/termitaria: the home of a colony of termites (white ants); it includes a vast maze of underground passages where the termites live, as well as a mound that is built above ground when the passages are dug out by the termites

Terrestrial: an animal that lives on land rather than water

Territory: an area which a creature considers to be his, and which he will defend against intruders of his own species

Veld: an area of natural vegetation that has not been cultivated

Wattle: Skin flaps, usually on the side of the face of certain birds e.g. Saddlebilled stork

INDEX

NOTES